EXPLORING THE ANCIENT
AND MEDIEVAL WORLDS

Empires, Crusaders, and Invasions Through the Middle Ages

Pliny O'Brian

Cavendish
Square
New York

Published in 2016 by Cavendish Square Publishing, LLC
243 5th Avenue, Suite 136, New York, NY 10016

Website: cavendishsq.com

This publication represents the opinions and views of the author based on his or her personal experience, knowledge, and
research. The information in this book serves as a general guide only. The author and publisher have used their best efforts
in preparing this book and disclaim liability rising directly or indirectly from the use and application of this book.

CPSIA Compliance Information: Batch #WS15CSQ

All websites were available and accurate when this book was sent to press.

Cataloging-in-Publication Data

O'Brian, Pliny.
Empires, crusaders, and invasions through the Middle Ages / by Pliny O'Brian.
p. cm. — (Exploring the ancient and medieval worlds)
Includes index.
ISBN 978-1-50260-679-2 (hardcover) ISBN 978-1-50260-680-8 (ebook)
1. Middle Ages — Juvenile literature. 2. Civilization, Medieval — Juvenile literature. I. O'Brian, Pliny. II. Title.
D117.O25 2016
909.07—d23

Editorial Director: David McNamara
Editor: Nathan Heidelberger
Copy Editor: Regina Murrell
Art Director: Jeff Talbot
Designer: Joseph Macri
Senior Production Manager: Jennifer Ryder-Talbot
Production Editor: Renni Johnson
Photo Research: J8 Media

The photographs in this book are used by permission and through the courtesy of: Apic/Hulton Archive/Getty Images,
cover; Preto Perola/Shutterstock.com, cover and throughout; Louvre, Paris, France/Peter Willi/Bridgeman Images, 4;
File:Nuremberg chronicles - Atilla, King of the Huns (CXXXVII).jpg/Wikimedia Commons, 7; Uploadalt File:Leo III
base gold solidus minted in Rome.jpg/Wikimedia Commons, 12; vvoe/Shutterstock.com, 13; Topkapi Palace Museum,
Istanbul, Turkey/Dost Yayinlari/Bridgeman Images, 16; PavleMarjanovic/Shutterstock.com,18; Public domain/
File:Thomas the Slav negotiates with the Arabs.jpg/Wikimedia Commons, 21; Public domain/File:Porphyrogenetus.
jpg/Wikimedia Commons, 23; Werner Forman/Universal Images Group/Getty Images, 25; Werner Forman/Universal
Images Group/Getty Images, 30; Apic/Hulton Archive/Getty Images, 32; Hulton Archive/Getty Images, 35; Art Media/
Print Collector/Getty Images, 38; Fine Art Images/Heritage Images/Getty Images, 41; De Agostini Picture Library/G.
Dagli Orti/Bridgeman Images, 44; Universal History Archive/Getty Images, 48; CM Dixon/Print Collector/Getty
Images, 51; Rimglow/iStockphoto.com, 56; National Museum of Iceland, Reykjavik, Iceland/Bridgeman Images, 59;
Torbenbrinker/File:L'AnseAuxMeadowsReconstr2.jpg/Wikimedia Commons, 60; Vereshchagin Dmitry/Shutterstock.
com, 62; Дар Ветер/File:1000 Rurik.jpg/Wikimedia Commons, 64; Fine Art Images/Heritage Images/Getty Images,
66; Public domain/File:Ivan vs khan.jpg/Wikimedia Commons, 71; Public domain/File:Alexander nevskiy ice battle3.
jpg/Wikimedia Commons, 72; Wolfgang Kaehler/LightRocket/Getty Images, 74; Bibliotheque Nationale, Paris, France/
Bridgeman Images, 77; Universal History Archive/Getty Images, 82; Public domain/File:Sacking of Suzdal by Batu
Khan.jpg/Wikimedia Commons, 84; Alfotokunst/Shutterstock.com, 86; Karol Kozlowski/Shutterstock.com, 87; Public
domain/File:The Inside of a Mosque, the Dervishes Dancing by William Hogarth (La Motraye's Travels, vol. I, pl. 16).
jpg/Wikimedia Commons, 91; Zereshk/File:Kharaghan.jpg/Wikimedia Commons, 92; File:DiezAlbumsFallOfBaghdad
a.jpg/Wikimedia Commons, 95; Public domain/File:DiezAlbumsStudyingTheKoran.jpg/Wikimedia Commons, 96;
Topkapi Palace Museum, Istanbul, Turkey/Bridgeman Images, 100; Public domain/File:Benjamin-Constant-The Entry of
Mahomet II into Constantinople-1876.jpg/Wikimedia Commons, 107; Public domain/File:John Sigismund of Hungary
with Suleiman the Magnificient in 1556.jpg/Wikimedia Commons, 111; Saiko3p/iStock/Thinkstock, 112; Public domain/
File:Battle of Preveza (1538).jpg/Wikimedia Commons, 114; Heini Schneebeli/Bridgeman Images, 114; Ji-Elle/File:Musée
national d'Ethiopie-Reconstitution de Lucy (1).jpg/Wikimedia Commons, 118; Pichugin Dmitry/Shutterstock.com,
120; Werner Forman/Universal Images Group/Getty Images, 126; Bibliotheque Nationale, Paris, France/Bridgeman
Images, 132; Werner Forman/Universal Images Group/Getty Images, 134; File:Pair of staffs, male and female couple,
Yoruba people, Honolulu Museum of Art, 5969.1.jpg/Wikimedia Commons, 136; Lynn Y/Shutterstock.com, 139; Public
domain/Bensusan Museum/File:King Moshoeshoe of the Basotho with his ministers.jpg/Wikimedia Commons, 140.

Printed in the United States of America

Contents

Chapter 1: The Rise of the Byzantine Empire   5

Chapter 2: Later Byzantine History   17

Chapter 3: The Holy Wars   33

Chapter 4: The Spread of the Vikings   49

Chapter 5: The Birth of Russia   63

Chapter 6: The Mongol Empire   75

Chapter 7: The Islamic World of the Middle Ages   89

Chapter 8: The Ottoman Empire   101

Chapter 9: The Cradle of Civilization   117

Chapter 10: The Tribes, Kingdoms, and Empires of Africa   127

Chronology   142
Glossary   146
Major Historical Figures   151
For Further Information   153
Index   154

Constantine the Great was responsible for many of the reforms that helped strengthen the Byzantine Empire.

CHAPTER ONE

The Rise of the Byzantine Empire

While the western portion of the Roman Empire suffered a series of barbarian invasions in the fifth century CE, the eastern portion, known today as the Byzantine Empire, thrived. Though partly a product of the chance combination of various circumstances, the flourishing of the Byzantine Empire can also be attributed to three well-calculated political maneuvers: the official recognition of Christianity, the reform of the currency, and the establishment of **Constantinople** (formerly **Byzantium**, now called Istanbul) as the empire's capital.

The early Byzantine rulers were also Roman emperors. Diocletian (ruled 284–305 CE) and **Constantine the Great** (sole emperor 324–337 CE) were both soldiers who imposed military discipline on a previously anarchic body politic; they even imposed their sense of order on religious affairs.

Constantine was particularly important because it was during his reign that the imperial Roman leadership system of co-emperors was finally acknowledged as unworkable and was replaced with a formal transfer of power within a single ruling family, often but not always from father to son. By the end of the fourth century CE, the dynastic principle was well established. Theodosius I was the last emperor to rule the unified Roman Empire. When he died in 395 CE, he divided his land between his sons, bequeathing the west to Honorius and the east to Arcadius.

Another of Constantine's great achievements was the regionalization of power. The success of local devolution and the separation of military authority from civilian government demonstrated that outlying provinces could be allowed a certain amount of political freedom without necessarily endangering the empire as a cohesive whole.

Constantine was a Christian convert who raised the status of his adopted faith to that of a "permitted religion." In the short term, it was a response to a popular trend; in the longer term, it helped to establish the religion permanently in southeastern Europe. Constantine also brought in a new currency, the gold solidus, which replaced the debased old denarius and remained the standard for centuries. Constantine transferred the capital of the empire from Rome to Byzantium, which he renamed Constantinople after himself in 330 CE.

The Goth Migration

In the second half of the fourth century CE, the **Huns** (a nomadic people who originated to the east of the Volga River) began attacking the Ostrogoths and the Visigoths (early Germanic peoples) and drove them west and south across the Danube River. Some of them sought refuge in the rapidly disintegrating Roman Empire, but they found exploitation at the hands of their new hosts. In 378 CE, they rose up and scored an important victory against the Romans at the Battle of Adrianople (modern Edirne, in European Turkey).

Later, the imperial rulers accepted the need to coexist with the Goths. Theodosius I (ruled 379–395 CE) granted the Goths lands and gave them the status of foederati (auxiliary soldiers). Having gained a measure of acceptance, the Goths later fought on the side of the Romans in several military campaigns.

In another significant development, Christianity became more than just an option. After 391 CE, the religion started to become a requirement. Tolerance of other faiths diminished; priests and politicians first defined heresy and then looked for ways to eradicate it. A new era of persecution was at hand.

Meanwhile, Constantinople became one of the world's most prosperous cities. Its wealth, based primarily on trade throughout the region, was boosted by a sudden influx of gold. The exact origin of the precious metal is unknown, but it may have come from newly discovered deposits in outlying regions or else from the looting of pagan temples.

Constantinople's wealth was a magnet for people from all over eastern Europe and the Mediterranean who flocked to the city in search of work and security; the fortress had earned a reputation for impregnability, and indeed, it remained unbreached until the **Fourth Crusade** in 1204 CE. Although there are no exact population figures, it is believed that, by the fifth century CE, Constantinople had at least two hundred thousand inhabitants and may have had as many as five hundred thousand, making it by far the most populous city in the world at the time. Having previously welcomed growth, the emperors became alarmed at the rate of increase and sought to restrict the number of residents by taxation and by imposing stricter requirements for citizenship.

The Hun Invasion

During the fifth century CE, the greatest threat to the Byzantine Empire came from the northeast, where the forces of **Attila the Hun** (ruled 434–453 CE) massed against it in the Balkans, in the Caucasus, and in parts of what is now Russia. Attila's troops captured and destroyed Singidunum (modern Belgrade, Serbia) in 441 CE and the cities of Nis and Sofia in 443 CE. Advancing southward, the Huns then set their sights on Constantinople, but having occupied the lands to the north and south of the city, Attila decided that his army—composed principally of archers—would be unable to storm it. The emperor Theodosius II (ruled 408–450 CE) negotiated a truce with the Huns and agreed to pay an annual tribute of 2,100 pounds of gold.

Attila the Hun posed a significant threat to the Byzantine Empire, but he failed to capture Constantinople.

The ensuing peace was uneasy, but Byzantine traders maximized the commercial opportunities; it appears that Constantinople benefited greatly from its subsequent trade with the Huns.

Independence from Rome

From 474 to 491 CE, the Byzantine Empire was ruled by Zeno, an Isaurian (from **Anatolia**, modern Turkey). The Byzantines had welcomed the Isaurian people to help them in their struggle against northern invaders, but once that danger had passed, they strove to rid themselves of Turkish influence. When Zeno died, his widow, Ariadne, married Anastasius, who succeeded to the imperial throne. The Isaurians tried to resist their loss of power, but their period of dominance was over, at least for the time being. Meanwhile, the Roman Empire finally disintegrated and the Byzantine Empire became an independent power.

Theological Debates

Although Christianity was now firmly established as the Byzantine religion, it was divided by internal controversies. The main point of contention was the teaching of Arius (circa 250–336 CE), a priest from Alexandria who argued that God and Christ were essentially different because God the Father had existed from the start of eternity, while God the Son was a child in time. Arius's theory had been rejected by the Christian church at the Council of Nicaea in 325 CE, but the idea—subsequently known as the **Arian heresy**—persisted in the fourth century CE and was definitively condemned only in 381 CE with promulgation at the Council of Aquileia of the doctrine that Father and Son were of one substance and thus coexistent.

However, the resolution of the Arian problem created a new theological difficulty as Christians argued about how to reconcile the human and divine elements of their deity. In the fifth century CE, two schools of thought emerged. One school, based in Alexandria, took the view that God the Father and God the Son were indistinguishable. That theory was known as Monophysitism. The other theory, known as Dyophysitism and based in Antioch, contended that both natures coexisted separately in Christ.

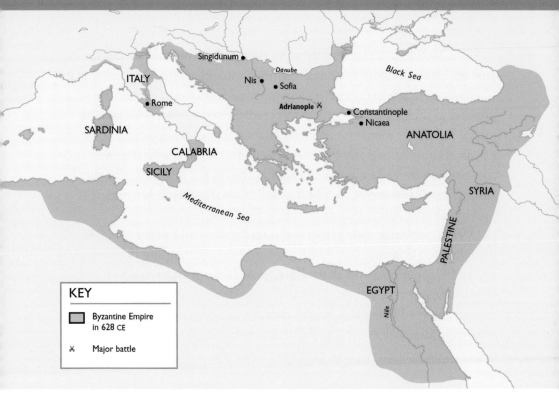

The argument fueled a struggle for power between the three main branches of the Christian church. In 428 CE, Nestorius, patriarch (archbishop) of Constantinople, ruled in favor of Dyophysitism. In Rome, Pope Leo I (ruled 440–461 CE) took the same view. Only Alexandria adopted Monophysitism as the true faith, and being in a minority, the Egyptian branch of Christianity gradually became sidelined.

Expansion and Reform

When the last emperor in Rome, Romulus Augustulus, was deposed by the German warrior Odoacer in 476 CE, the eastern part of the old empire comprised the Balkan Peninsula, much of southwestern Asia, Palestine, Egypt, and northeastern Africa. When the emperor Justinian (ruled 527–565 CE) came to the throne in Constantinople, he extended Byzantine power even farther. The Byzantine armies retained the military cohesion and discipline that had been features of the armies of the Roman Empire, and Justinian employed generals of genius such as Belisarius. Byzantine forces took northern Africa, Italy, part of Spain, and the Mediterranean islands of Sicily and Sardinia. At its peak, around 550 CE, Justinian's empire almost encircled the Mediterranean.

Justinian's achievements as a conqueror were matched by his prowess as a legislator. He sought to eradicate corruption and provide justice for all his subjects, objectives that could not be achieved without a radical reorganization of the legal system. He produced a new constitution in 529 CE and a classic handbook for law students, the *Institutiones* (*Institutes*), in 534 CE. In 535 CE, he banned the sale of provincial governorships, a previously frequent practice.

While Justinian was preoccupied with those and other projects, he delegated domestic administration to two outstanding deputies, John of Cappadocia and Peter Barsymes. Their primary task—to raise sufficient revenue to maintain imperial territories—was not straightforward because many of the frontier provinces were too poor to sustain themselves. The two ministers solved the problem by taxing imports, particularly spices, perfumes, and silk.

The Nika Revolt

The taxation and the emperor's war on corruption were deeply unpopular with the inhabitants of Constantinople. In 532 CE, the city's two main political factions—the Blues and the Greens—united in an uprising known as the **Nika Revolt**, from the Greek word for "victory." The rebels ran riot, setting fire to several public buildings and part of the imperial palace. When no one confronted them, they called for Justinian to be replaced by Hypatius, the nephew of the late emperor Anastasius (ruled 491–518 CE). For a time, it looked as if the rebels might prevail, but then troops led by Belisarius intervened and restored order by massacring the insurgents. Hypatius was later put to death.

Threatened Borders

Justinian laid the foundation of the Byzantine Empire, but he did not complete its construction. He left enormous challenges for his successors. The key strategic problems lay at the frontiers of the Byzantine Empire; Italy and the Balkans were still periodically threatened by barbarian invaders, while the eastern borders of the empire were confronted with a succession of threats, first from the

Persian Sassanid Empire, then from Arabs who were spreading **Islam** by the sword, and finally from central Asian Turkic peoples who themselves created powerful empires. By the end of the sixth century CE, the Byzantine Empire had surrendered most of its territory in northern Italy to the Lombards, and the Balkans were ravaged several times over, first by Avar raiders from the Caucasus and later by Slavic tribes who moved in to claim great swathes of undefended Byzantine territory.

The assassination of the emperor Maurice (ruled 582–602 CE) ushered in a period of civil strife in the Byzantine Empire. In 610 CE, a soldier named Heraclius seized the throne from Maurice's successor, the incompetent and despotic Phocas. Sensing a power vacuum, the Avars and Persians promptly invaded the Byzantine Empire. In 622 CE, Heraclius counterattacked, dispatching the Avars back to central Europe and driving the Persians from Anatolia, Egypt, and Syria. In 628 CE, Heraclius invaded Persia itself.

The next major challenge to the Byzantine Empire came from the Arab armies that swarmed westward from the Arabian Peninsula. The Arabs enjoyed great early success, defeating Persian forces, conquering the Sassanid Empire, and taking over many of the eastern provinces of the Byzantine Empire, including Syria and Egypt. They attacked Constantinople itself in the 670s CE, but in the face of ferocious opposition, they were unable to surmount the city walls.

Leo III

In the early eighth century CE, the Byzantine Empire was attacked simultaneously on three fronts by the Slavs, the **Bulgars**, and the Arabs. From 717 to 718 CE, Constantinople itself was besieged. The emperor Theodosius III was overthrown in 717 CE by his leading general, who took the throne as Leo III. Leo and his family became known as the Isaurian dynasty, but unlike Zeno, they came from Syria rather than Anatolia. Having fought off the Arabs on land and at sea, Leo established a state that remained stable for the following three hundred years. The frontiers of the eighth-century CE Byzantine Empire were secured by an army of up to 150,000 men, most of whom served in cataphracts (units of armored archers on horseback) that were deployed along the eastern edges of Anatolia and Thrace (Asia Minor and northern Greece).

This gold solidus bears the face of Emperor Leo III.

Having secured the frontiers of his empire, Leo set about modernizing its legal system. In 726 CE, he issued a new code, the *Ecloga*, which revised the precepts established in the sixth century CE by the emperor Justinian. The *Ecloga* paid particular attention to property rights and the regulation of marriage along Christian lines. It also reduced the maximum penalty for several offenses from death to amputation and mutilation. In order to reduce corruption, Leo made judges salaried employees of the state rather than volunteers, so that they would be less susceptible to bribery.

Iconodules and Iconoclasts

When Leo turned his attention to religion, he ordered the forced baptism of all Byzantine Jews and various Christian sects that he decreed heretical. Then, in 730 CE, the emperor introduced **iconoclasm**, the measure for which he is principally remembered.

At the time, many Christians worshipped images of God and holy relics (sacred objects, such as pieces of wood that were believed to come from the cross on which Jesus was crucified). Such people were known as iconodules. Other Christians, however, believed that such practices were sacrilegious. They were known as iconoclasts, from the Greek word for "destroyers of images."

For many years, the two forms of worship coexisted, but mutual tolerance ended abruptly after Leo made iconoclasm imperial policy. Leo's proclamation gave the iconoclasts authority to raid churches and remove and destroy all the sacred images they found there. The campaign began in earnest with the demolition of the great gold icon of Christ beside the Bronze Gate that led to the royal palace in Constantinople. The act caused outrage among Leo's subjects. The commander of the demolition squad was attacked and killed by

The simple cross adorning the dome of Hagia Irene, one of Istanbul's oldest churches, is a rare surviving example of iconoclastic church decoration.

a group of women. Undeterred, Leo persevered with his campaign. When Germanus I, the patriarch of Constantinople, condemned the attacks, Leo had him removed from office and replaced by one of his own sympathizers, Anastasius. For minor opponents of iconoclasm, the penalties were harsher. Clerics who tried to resist the emperor's will were beaten and thrown in jail.

In 734 CE, Leo issued a decree that not only icons but all representations of the human figure in religious art should be destroyed and that any failure to do so would be harshly punished. At first, the decree created an uproar, but eventually the churchmen of the empire agreed that Leo's controversial decision should be upheld. All icons were smashed, and all statues were removed from their plinths. The controversy over the worship of icons then abated, but it resurfaced periodically thereafter and remained an important issue in Byzantine society until 847 CE.

Leo encountered further opposition from Rome, where popes Gregory II (ruled 715–731 CE) and Gregory III (ruled 731–741 CE) warned the emperor against any attempt to implement iconoclasm in Byzantine territories in southern Italy. Leo retaliated by cutting financial aid to the papacy and decreeing that churches in Sicily and Calabria should break with Rome and come under the jurisdiction of the eastern patriarch. The vehemence of Leo's response alarmed the papacy, which was forced to turn to the Frankish rulers for support. As a result, there was a westward shift in the balance of power that gradually weakened Byzantine influence on the Italian Peninsula. The enmities created by the iconoclasm struggle disrupted the Byzantine Empire for more than a hundred years.

The Decline of Roman Influence

During the early Middle Ages, the Byzantine Empire became less Roman and more Greek, even though, as late as the seventh century CE, the emperors still addressed their subjects as *Romaioi* (Romans). Foreigners called Byzantine citizens *Graeci* (Greeks) because Greek was the language used for all the empire's administrative, scientific, and educational purposes. In addition to Greek, Coptic (the language of ancient Egypt), Syriac, and Armenian were among a host of tongues that were widely spoken in the Byzantine Empire. However, Latin was no longer used, and the abandonment of the language of Rome was an eloquent symbol of the division of the old empire.

By the reign of Leo III, Byzantine emperors were no longer referred to by the Latin titles caesar or imperator. Instead, they were called basileus, the Greek word for "king" or "emperor." The basileus was the source of all secular law and the center of political authority. He also played a key role in religious matters, thus lending imperial weight to church doctrine. In addition to making military and political appointments, the basileus presided over the selection of the patriarch of Constantinople.

This sixteenth-century CE map depicts Constantinople as it appeared in the Middle Ages.

CHAPTER TWO

Later Byzantine History

The Byzantine Empire reached its apex in the eleventh century CE, on the heels of more than a hundred years of territorial expansion. The Battle of Manzikert in 1071 CE, in which the Byzantines suffered a decisive defeat against the Turks, marked the beginning of the end for the empire. The sack of Constantinople at the hands of European crusaders in 1204 CE brought additional troubles, and by the mid-fifteenth century CE, the empire had completely dissolved.

While Leo III had rescued the Byzantine Empire during a period of great crisis (717–718 CE), the emperor left a legacy of discord by banning religious images (icons), a policy known as iconoclasm. Over the following three centuries, the conflicts generated by the dispute over iconoclasm were gradually resolved. Leo's immediate successor, his son Constantine V (ruled 741–775 CE) upheld the controversial policy, but subsequent emperors were more lenient. Constantine's son, Leo IV (ruled 775–780 CE), married into an aristocratic Athenian family. His wife, Irene, was ambitious, scheming, and cruel. She was an iconodule (one who believes that icons are a means of achieving a religious experience). Despite the official edicts against the veneration of images, her husband raised no objection to her method of worship.

Empress Irene

In the beginning, Irene stayed in the background. Then, in 780 CE, Leo was incapacitated by a virulent fever. When he died in September of that year, leaving a ten-year-old son, Irene lost no time in securing the regency for herself. Although her child was nominally the emperor Constantine VI, Irene was the power behind the throne for the next eleven years.

With her newly acquired authority, Irene sought to promote the veneration of icons. When the patriarch (bishop) of Constantinople resigned in 784 CE, Irene appointed her secretary, Tarasius, in his place. Following Irene's iconodule policy, Tarasius decided that relations with Rome must be restored. Accordingly, western churchmen were invited to an ecumenical council at Nicaea (modern Iznik, Turkey) in 787 CE for the purpose of condemning iconoclasm. The council duly did so, with the proviso that icons were to be venerated rather than worshipped.

Empress Irene, shown here in a mosaic from Istanbul's Hagia Sofia, was a controversial leader.

The regent's interference in religious affairs aroused great ill feeling among the Byzantine people. Young Constantine VI became a rallying point for their discontent. When Irene uncovered a conspiracy against her, she put Constantine in prison and decreed that every soldier in the army should swear a personal oath of allegiance to her. However, the Armeniakoi, an Armenian regiment of great military and political importance, mutinied. Constantine was proclaimed sole ruler. Irene was held under guard in her palace, and Constantine was crowned emperor.

In spite of his initial popularity, Constantine soon alienated most of his supporters. His foreign policy was a disaster. He concluded a humiliating peace treaty with invading Arabs and fled the battlefield during a confrontation with the Bulgars. When Constantine divorced his first wife and married another woman, even the iconodules lost patience with him. Irene was recalled to court, and behind the scenes, she reassembled her supporters and prepared to form a new government.

One day, when Constantine was out riding, he was taken prisoner by a party of soldiers and brought back to the palace. His mother then ordered that his eyes should be gouged out. The emperor died shortly afterward from his injuries.

Irene's subsequent conduct did nothing to improve her reputation as a cruel despot. Rather than following tradition and choosing a husband to rule, she had herself crowned empress. She made a bid for popularity by lowering taxes, but that merely crippled the empire's finances.

The Coronation of Charlemagne

On Christmas Day of 800 CE, Pope Leo III crowned the king of the Franks, **Charlemagne**, as Holy Roman emperor. There had been no emperor in the west for more than four hundred years. The coronation had enormous symbolic significance; by performing it, the pope was claiming supremacy over the emperor. Constantinople was rocked by the news, feeling that the pope had acted with unparalleled arrogance.

Soon, another event caused even greater consternation. Charlemagne proposed marriage to Irene, and the empress expressed her readiness to accept. The union made sound political sense. For Charlemagne, it was an opportunity to unite the western and eastern empires under his own rule. For Irene, it was a chance to save her empire from bankruptcy. The wedding never took place, however. Irene lost her throne in 802 CE in a bloodless palace revolution led by Nicephorus, the minister of finance. She was exiled to the island of Lesbos and died in the following year. Irene was the last ruler of the Isaurian dynasty.

Rapid Successions

The new emperor, Nicephorus I, did his best to repair the economic and political damage caused by his predecessor. He established diplomatic relations with Charlemagne, put the imperial finances in order, and organized military campaigns against the pagan Bulgars who were invading from the north. For a time, the campaigns were successful. However, in July of 811 CE, Nicephorus, his army, and his son Stauracius were ambushed by Bulgars. Nicephorus was killed, along with many of his soldiers; Stauracius was severely injured and left with a broken back.

For two months, Stauracius tried to govern from his sickbed, but when it became clear that the Byzantine Empire could not be ruled effectively by an invalid, he was persuaded to abdicate in favor of his brother-in-law Michael.

As emperor, Michael turned out to be weak-willed and profligate with money. Nevertheless, it was during his short reign that the eastern and western emperors signed a treaty, known as the Pax Nicephori, which upheld both rulers' rights to imperial status. Each emperor was free to pursue his own policies while respecting those of the other.

Meanwhile, the Bulgars, led by Khan Krum, were posing a renewed threat. At the Battle of Versinicia in June of 813 CE, Michael confronted the invaders with a force of mainly Macedonian and Anatolian troops. The Anatolians deserted, leaving the Macedonian contingent to be slaughtered. Michael escaped to Constantinople, where he abdicated. The throne was taken by an Armenian commander named Leo, who had been in charge of the Anatolians. Michael was banished to a monastery, where he died in 841 CE.

The Council of Orthodoxy

Leo V (ruled 813–820 CE) was a moderate iconoclast. He worked to restore the economy and the military organization of the Byzantine Empire. His reign was ended by a conspiracy. A close assistant to the emperor was arrested, but with the help of his guard, the prisoner managed to get word to his fellow plotters, and on the following morning, disguised as monks, they infiltrated the palace chapel and assassinated Leo during a service. With chains still around his feet, Michael II was crowned emperor.

The new ruler's first great challenge was a rebellion in Anatolia (part of modern Turkey) led by Thomas the Slav, who had once been a friend and fellow officer of the new basileus (emperor) and his predecessor. Although elderly, Thomas was a charismatic figure who won the support of disgruntled members of Byzantine society. He recruited a huge army of dissatisfied farmers and adventurers and, with Muslim support, laid siege to the capital, Constantinople. The people of Constantinople resisted, and eventually, the Bulgars, who had made a peace treaty with the Byzantines, offered to help. Early in 823 CE,

This twelfth-century CE manuscript shows Thomas the Slav negotiating for Arab support of his rebellion against the Byzantines.

a Bulgarian horde attacked the besieging army and cut it to pieces. Thomas escaped, but later in the year, he was captured, brought before the emperor, and sentenced to have his hands and feet cut off before being impaled on a stake.

During the ninth century CE, the Byzantine Empire engaged in a series of wars against the Muslim **caliphate** in Baghdad and the Bulgars in the Balkans, in Italy, and at sea. The power of the Muslim caliphate was waning, however, and the Byzantine armies remained strong. Under Michael's son, Theophilus (ruled 829–842 CE), Constantinople prospered as never before.

Theophilus embarked on an extravagant building program and decorated his own palace in lavish Arab style. Yet, despite his admiration for all things Islamic, Theophilus was forced to fight constant border wars against the **caliph**. Although the emperor was himself an iconoclast, he did not inquire too closely into what his subjects did in their own homes. Indeed, his own wife, Theodora, took the view that artistic representation of the sacred was acceptable.

On the death of Theophilus, Theodora took over the government on behalf of their three-year-old son, Michael. As empress, one of

Theodora's first concerns was to get rid of iconoclasm. In 843 CE, she convened the Council of Orthodoxy, which declared that the veneration of icons was now legitimate and branded leading iconoclasts, living and dead, as heretics. (Theodora stipulated, however, that her late husband should not be one of those denounced.) That decision led to the end of iconoclasm in 847 CE.

On reaching adulthood, Theodora's son became the emperor Michael III. He was weak and indecisive and preferred a life of leisure to the responsibilities of office. For a time, Michael delegated his duties to his uncle, Bardas, while he himself went drinking with a friend named Basil, an ambitious Armenian peasant. Basil made himself indispensable to Michael and rose to become lord chamberlain. In 866 CE, Basil arranged to have Bardas assassinated. Almost immediately afterward, Michael appointed Basil as co-emperor.

Michael then declined into alcohol dependency and became an embarrassment to his co-emperor. On the night of September 27, 867 CE, Basil and a gang of accomplices entered the imperial bedchamber and hacked Michael to death while he slept.

The Macedonian Dynasty

As sole emperor, Basil I founded the Macedonian dynasty, which ruled for more than two hundred years. His first contact with the man who would make him co-emperor had been through his work as a stable hand in the imperial stables. However, although Basil was illiterate and uneducated, he proved to be a highly capable emperor.

During his reign (867–886 CE), Basil strengthened his army and won important victories over Muslim forces, particularly in southern Italy. He reformed the administration of government and began an overhaul of the legal system—eventually completed by his son, Leo VI (ruled 886–912 CE).

Leo's son, Constantine VII, was only eight years old when he inherited the throne. For a while, his mother, the empress Zoe, acted as regent, but her unpopular policies provoked an uprising. In 920 CE, a Byzantine admiral, Romanus Lecapenus, seized power and was crowned co-emperor with Constantine. Having consolidated his position by forcing a marriage between his daughter and Constantine,

The Byzantine emperors claimed that their authority was invested in them by God. This tenth-century CE woodcarving depicts Christ crowning Constantine VII.

Romanus I ruled for almost a quarter of a century (920–944 CE) before he retired to a monastery, leaving Constantine to rule alone.

Constantine VII had a gentle, retiring nature and devoted much of his life to literary pursuits. While others maneuvered for power, Constantine was a patron of scholarship and wrote books on various aspects of government. He was highly capable, however. Not only did he run an effective administration, he also inspired a cultural renaissance in the empire. He sponsored the recopying of ancient manuscripts, the writing of new reference works, and a revival of the study of science, mathematics, and literature. Constantine preferred law to war and left military matters to his generals, who made significant inroads into the Islamic states of Mesopotamia and Syria.

After his father-in-law Romanus I was ousted from power, Constantine continued the efforts they had begun jointly to protect the tenants of small farms. He also maintained the contact that he and Romanus had established with the Russians, whom they hoped to convert to Christianity.

Constantine's successor, Romanus II, died in 963 CE after a short reign. His widow, Theophano, had the right to give her hand in marriage, and the crown with it, to the man of her choice. She chose Nicephorus Phocas, who had been Constantine's general and had commanded the army in the reconquest of Crete in 961 CE. Yet, in spite of his military successes, Nicephorus represented all the things that were detested by the cultured citizens of Constantinople. He was uneducated, coarse, and tyrannical. He also lived an ascetic life, free of any luxuries. Ignoring all opposition, Nicephorus marched on the capital city, married Theophano, and ascended the imperial throne.

Nicephorus believed in the justice of the holy war against the Muslims. He put all the resources of the empire into the service of the military. Every Byzantine victory was followed almost at once by fresh campaigns that required new recruits and new taxes.

Nicephorus considered the monasteries to be too rich for the good of their monks, so he decided to confiscate their property. That initiative antagonized the clergy, and relations between church and state deteriorated further when the emperor decreed that every Byzantine soldier killed in battle should be made a saint. In 969 CE, palace officials conspired against Nicephorus. They were aided by the

The Bulgarians

In the seventh century CE, Bulgar tribesmen of Turkic origin invaded Lower Moesia, a Balkan province of the Byzantine Empire. By the ninth century CE, they had formed their own empire, and their king, Khan Krum (ruled 803–814 CE), resoundingly defeated a Byzantine army in 811 CE and almost took Constantinople in 813 CE.

In this eleventh-century CE manuscript, Byzantine forces repel the Bulgarian siege of Thessalonki.

In 864 CE, Boris I (ruled 852–889 CE) was persuaded by the Byzantine emperor Michael III to make Christianity the official religion of Bulgaria. When, in 870 CE, Pope Adrian II refused to grant Bulgaria its own bishopric, Boris committed Bulgaria to Eastern Orthodoxy.

Boris's son, Simeon, brought Bulgaria to the zenith of its power through superb administration and successful military campaigns, most notably against the Byzantines and the Magyars. In 925 CE, Simeon declared himself czar of the Greeks as well as the Bulgars and went on to conquer Serbia the following year. However, he introduced Byzantine culture into his own empire and sponsored advances in education. His reign saw the first written works in the Bulgarian language and the adoption of the Cyrillic alphabet. Greatly influenced by its dominant Slavic population, Bulgaria became the center of Slavic culture in Europe during the tenth and eleventh centuries CE.

After Simeon's death in 927 CE, Bulgaria's fortunes declined. In 970 CE, its capital and the royal family were captured by Russians. The Byzantine emperor **John I Tzimisces** intervened, forcing the Russians out of the country. Although John I promised to restore the young czar, Boris, to his throne, he had no intention of doing so. Soon after his successful campaign, John persuaded Boris to abdicate, and Bulgaria temporarily became a Byzantine province.

empress Theophano, who had fallen in love with John I Tzimisces (a companion-in-arms of the emperor) and wanted to marry him.

On the night of December 10, the conspirators, led by John I Tzimisces, crept into the imperial bedchamber where the emperor (who rejected the comfort of the bed as a self-indulgence) lay asleep on the floor. They kicked him awake and then stabbed him to death.

The throne was then seized by John I Tzimisces, who was forced by the patriarch of Constantinople to banish Theophano as a condition of his coronation. One of John's first acts was to intervene in Bulgaria (see siedebar, p. 25) in 970 CE with the result that Bulgaria became part of the Byzantine Empire. John I also campaigned vigorously against the Islamic states in Mesopotamia and Syria from 972 to 975 CE. In 972 CE, John arranged the marriage of Theophano to Otto, son of Henry I of Germany, in an effort to improve relations between the Byzantine and Holy Roman empires.

John I Tzimisces died in 976 CE and was succeeded by Basil II, the son of Romanus II. Basil ruled jointly with his younger brother, Constantine VIII, who was happy to play a subordinate role in affairs of state. During Basil's reign, which lasted until 1025 CE, the Byzantine army regained territory in southeastern Anatolia, Greece, Macedonia, and Thrace. Meanwhile, the Byzantine navy extended imperial power and established trading links in lands bordering the Mediterranean and Black Seas.

Basil conquered Armenia, which was a threat to Byzantium from the east, and finally subdued the Bulgars, who, after the death of John I Tzimisces, had claimed independence under the leadership of a self-proclaimed czar named Samuel. Basil waged war on the Bulgars for twenty years. He finally defeated Samuel in 1014 CE, and he owes his nickname, "the Bulgar slayer," to the savage way in which he dealt with the remnants of Samuel's army. The eyes of fifteen thousand Bulgarian prisoners were gouged out, although one soldier in every hundred was allowed to keep one eye in order to be able to lead the others home. In midwinter, Basil threw the blinded army out of the country. When he saw his forces hobbling home, Samuel had a heart attack and died. Basil finally incorporated Bulgaria into the Byzantine Empire in 1018 CE.

Empress Zoe

Basil died in 1025 CE, leaving the Byzantine Empire in a strong position on all its frontiers. His aged brother, Constantine VIII, took over as sole ruler until his own death three years later. On his deathbed, Constantine sanctioned the marriage of his daughter Zoe to Romanus, the prefect of Constantinople. Within a few days, the two were crowned emperor and empress. The union was not a happy one, however. Romanus III took a mistress; the furious empress then had the emperor drowned in his bath. On the following day, she married her lover, the notorious pleasure-seeking Michael, making him emperor Michael IV. After Michael's death in 1041 CE, Zoe adopted Michael's nephew as her son and heir, and he was crowned Michael V. Trying to assert his authority, Michael had Zoe banished, a move that sparked a popular uprising. The empress was hastily recalled, but the mob was now out of control, and Constantinople endured one of the bloodiest days in its history. Michael lost his throne and had his eyes gouged out.

Zoe married again. Her new husband, a high-ranking official, became Constantine IX. As emperor, Constantine's most striking characteristic was his indecisiveness. His death, in 1055 CE, heralded a period of upheaval.

Defeat at Manzikert

The twelve years following the death of Constantine IX saw a series of emperors. Then, on January 1, 1068 CE, an outstanding general was crowned as Romanus IV. The new basileus had been chosen partly because Constantinople's senior aristocrats and bureaucrats were alarmed by the weakness of the empire's armed forces in the face of new threats. Both on land and at sea, Byzantine strength had declined in the eleventh century CE, while the very basis of the army—a regional network of units known as *themes*, each with its own leader—was failing to produce the number of soldiers required, because the men had been allowed to buy their way out of service and work on farms instead.

The new threats faced by the empire came from the Normans in Italy and the **Seljuk** Turks, a central Asian people who had established an empire that included Iraq and much of Syria. In 1071 CE, Romanus IV mounted a large campaign to repel the Turks from eastern Anatolia. The two armies met near the town of Manzikert. During the ensuing battle, it seems likely that a large part of the Byzantine army was ordered to retreat as part of a deliberate conspiracy. The withdrawal of troops left the vanguard, in which Romanus was fighting, unsupported. As the Turks attacked, the Byzantine line broke and their troops were massacred. Romanus was captured and taken to the camp of the Turkish commander, **Alp Arslan**, where he was treated courteously in accordance with Islamic rules of hospitality. A peace treaty was concluded, in which Romanus conceded some territories and agreed to pay a substantial ransom and an annual tribute. Romanus was then set free, but on his return to Constantinople, he was deposed by Michael VII, whose family may have conspired against Romanus at the Battle of Manzikert. Michael refused to honor the treaty with Alp Arslan, inspiring fresh incursions by the Turks and leading to the loss of much of Anatolia. Where the Turks did not conquer, they ravaged so thoroughly that the Anatolian population did not recover for more than a century, and the greatest recruiting ground for the empire's armies was laid to waste. The Battle of Manzikert had lasting repercussions and marked the beginning of the end of the Byzantine Empire.

The Fall of the Empire

After the Battle of Manzikert, the Byzantine Empire was assailed on all sides by enemies and came close to ruin. It was saved, as it had been before, by the strength of the fortifications of Constantinople itself, which repelled successive waves of invaders, and by a brilliant military emperor, **Alexius Comnenus** (ruled 1081–1118 CE). Comnenus restored the empire's position in the Balkans by taking maximum advantage of the opportunities presented by the **First Crusade**. The defeat of Turkish forces by Christian knights enabled the emperor to reclaim many former Byzantine possessions in the region. Under Alexius Comnenus's two immediate successors—John Comnenus (ruled 1118–1143 CE) and Manuel Comnenus (ruled 1143–1180 CE)—Constantinople again exerted a major influence in the eastern Mediterranean. Exploiting limited resources to their full potential, the two emperors successfully played all their adversaries and rivals against each other. Their strategies enabled them to prevail against the Seljuk Turks in Anatolia, the crusader states in Palestine and Syria, the Normans in Italy, the maritime might of Venice in the Adriatic and the eastern Mediterranean, and the emerging powers of Bulgaria and Hungary in eastern Europe.

The Byzantine revival was brought to an end in 1185 CE, when the last of the Comnenus dynasty was deposed and murdered. The demise of the empire as a great power was now inevitable. The leaders of the Fourth Crusade agreed to a demand from the Venetians, who were transporting them to Palestine, that they attack Constantinople. The city, which had withstood so many attacks, was taken in 1204 CE and became the center of a new Latin empire that lasted for fifty-seven years. Various Byzantine leaders formed states in other areas of the greatly diminished empire.

After decades of warfare, Michael VIII reestablished the Byzantine Empire in 1261 CE by recapturing Constantinople from his original base in Nicaea. However, the state was a mere shadow of its former self. It survived only by allying itself with the Turkish states in Anatolia and by agreeing to their sovereignty over it. By 1350 CE, the Byzantine Empire consisted of no more than Constantinople itself, Thessaloniki, and parts of southern Greece. Although Constantinople repelled sieges by the Ottoman Turks in 1398–1399 CE and 1422 CE, the city was unable to withstand a further Ottoman onslaught in 1453 CE.

Constantine XI, the final Byzantine basileus, made a desperate attempt to reverse the decline. He went so far as to align the empire with western Christendom, swearing an oath to the church of Rome. European help never came, however, and the emperor died in 1453 CE while trying, to no avail, to save the once impregnable city of Constantinople from a Turkish invasion. The last vestige of the Byzantine Empire, the Black Sea port of Trebizond, fell to the Ottomans in 1461 CE. The empire was officially no more.

Byzantine Art and Architecture

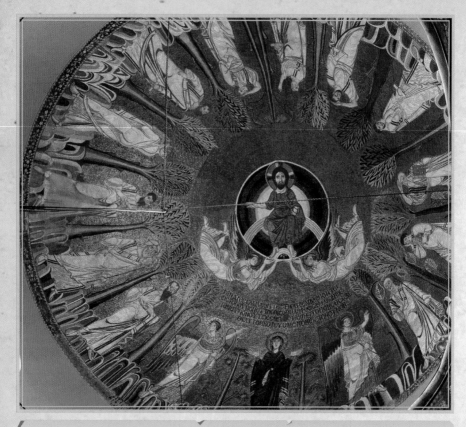

The dome of Hagia Sophia in Thessaloniki, dating from the ninth century CE, is a typical example of the Macedonian Renaissance style. The mosaic places Christ at the apex of the dome, with other religious figures beneath him.

The end of iconoclasm in 847 CE heralded an outstanding period in Byzantine art as painters celebrated the new freedom of religious expression by producing a rich array of new icons, most of which were flat images produced with oil paint, mosaics, gold, and ivory.

Because it coincided with the Macedonian dynasty, this period in Byzantine art is known as the Macedonian Renaissance. Artists of the period returned to the classical Hellenistic style as the model for their paintings. However, because it was not acceptable to portray the naked human body in religious work, they adopted the Greek practice of clothing their figures in clinging drapery that merely hinted at the body beneath. The style is known as damp-fold. The artists also used abstract patterns or networks of lines to indicate the three-dimensional nature of their figures, rather than shading techniques that would have given a stronger sense of volume. Such artistic conventions—which were developed to conform with the requirements of the church—remained characteristic of Byzantine art for centuries.

Mosaic decoration followed a typical pattern that was closely linked to the predominant style of church architecture. Although broadly inspired by the structure of the famous Hagia Sophia in Constantinople (a great dome set over a square base), Middle Byzantine churches tended to be smaller and more intimate than their original models. While the earlier buildings had used huge curved arches (called pendentives) set on the sides of the square to support the domed roof, churches constructed during the Middle Byzantine period incorporated smaller arches (called squinches) at the corners of the square to hold the dome. The architects also added four equilateral areas to the sides of the square to form the arms of a cross. This cross-in-the-square became a common pattern, particularly in the eleventh century CE .

The interior of most Byzantine churches was covered with mosaic or painted images of sacred people and events. Their position indicated the importance of the subject portrayed. Christ, always with a full beard, commanded the center of the dome, looking down on all creation. On the rim of the dome and high on the walls were biblical scenes and pictorial anecdotes from the life of the Virgin Mary, who was venerated as the mother of God. Important saints were shown on major structural supports, while less important ones appeared low down on the walls. In the semi-dome of the apse (a projection usually on the eastern side of the church), Mary was typically shown carrying the infant Jesus.

Peter the Hermit assembled the largest—and most notoriously unruly—popular army of the First Crusade.

CHAPTER THREE

The Holy Wars

When he called for the First Crusade in 1095 CE, Pope Urban II (ruled 1088–1099 CE) was sending medieval Europe into over two centuries of religious conflict. A series of Christian military campaigns, the crusades were mostly intended to remove the Holy Land—and especially Jerusalem—from Islamic control. Some of these Holy Wars, however, were aimed at Muslims in Spain, or at the pagan populations of eastern Europe. One, the **Albigensian** Crusade (see sidebar, pages 44–45), was conducted much closer to home—it was an attempt to quell heretical beliefs in southern France. The crusades were never fully successful.

At the heart of the Holy Wars lay a deep religious impulse that seldom manifested itself benevolently. On the contrary, the crusades were typically characterized by enormous savagery toward non-Christians (and sometimes other Christians), and they were always overlaid by the personal and political ambitions of their leaders. The crusades also had social motivations. Rising population levels and the need for the younger sons of nobles to establish their own fiefdoms are widely regarded as two of the main reasons why many Europeans found interest in the Holy Wars. The crusades had no single main cause; there were many complex reasons for them.

The Council of Clermont

The First Crusade was proclaimed in 1095 CE by Pope Urban II at the Council of Clermont, a city in France. There were two ostensible reasons for the pope's announcement. The first reason was that Christian pilgrims were encountering problems in the Holy Land. Pilgrimage had become an important part of religious life by the late eleventh century CE, but Palestine was under the control of Seljuk Turks who made Christians unwelcome in Jerusalem. The second reason was related to the split that had happened between the eastern and western Christian churches in 1054 CE. In 1071 CE, the Seljuks defeated Byzantine forces at the Battle of Manzikert and threatened Constantinople itself. The Byzantine emperor Alexius Comnenus then called on western Christendom for help. Alexius worked on detente with the Latin Christians, and Urban was anxious to restore relations between the two churches. As a result, Urban finally rescinded the excommunication under which Rome had held Byzantium since the original schism. In return, Alexius reopened the Latin churches in Constantinople.

Pope Urban II was keen on providing armed assistance, which he saw as a means for reuniting the whole Christian church while reclaiming the Holy Land for Christendom. At Clermont, he outlined his plan for a war to end Muslim control over Jerusalem. Urban appealed to Christians to turn their warrior spirit to a holy cause. He called the war a crusade, taking the name from the Latin word *crux* (cross). His proposal was immediately acclaimed. "*Deus le vult!*" ("God wills it!"), shouted the vast crowd assembled in a field outside Clermont.

The People's Crusade

The first bishop to respond to the pope's challenge was Adhemar of Le Puy (France). Almost immediately, several hundred people followed Adhemar's example and pledged themselves to the cause. The pope appointed Adhemar commander in chief of the First Crusade and directed the other bishops to return home and start recruiting. The idea was that groups of crusaders, each with their own leader and financing, would converge on Constantinople and join forces with the Byzantines. Together, they would retake Anatolia (part of modern Turkey) from the Seljuks and then proceed to Syria and Palestine.

Throughout Europe, the popular response to Urban's call was enthusiastic. The enlistment effort began at once. It largely followed the pope's plan, but Urban had not anticipated the excitement it would arouse among the common people of Europe. Peasants and city folk, merchants and adventurers alike sewed crosses on their clothing and joined in what became known as the People's Crusade.

The largest popular army was recruited and led by a preacher from northern France named Peter the Hermit (ca. 1050–1115 CE). Peter assembled an undisciplined mob of some forty thousand people in France and Germany. With no equipment and few provisions, they set off eastward, plundering as they went. In Hungary, they attacked the town of Semlin, killing many of its inhabitants. Their onward rampage continued with many skirmishes until Byzantine troops were sent to oppose them at Nis (a city in modern Serbia) and many

This fifteenth-century CE manuscript shows Pope Urban II presiding over the Council of Clermont in 1095 CE.

crusaders were killed. The Christian forces reached Constantinople in August of 1096 CE with their numbers greatly reduced.

Alexius Comnenus was horrified by this response to his appeal for help. It was clear to him that this rabble army could not remain in the city, where it had already begun to plunder and rape. Alexius arranged for the army to be shipped to Anatolia, where it marched straight into a Turkish ambush. Most of the crusaders were killed, and the survivors were sold into slavery.

Jewish Persecution

The crusaders' recruitment drive in the Rhineland met with particular success. Large numbers of Christians accepted the pilgrim's cross, but the armies in which they enlisted fell into the hands of profiteering robber barons. They were further distracted from their mission to the

Holy Land by potential targets much closer to home. They turned against the Jews, who were persecuted because they had not been baptized.

After plundering Jewish possessions, the Christian army of the Rhineland headed east in the wake of Peter the Hermit. They did not get far, however. Having learned from experience what a crusading army could do, the Hungarian king closed his borders to the invaders, who then dispersed. Many of them died before they could return home.

Five Armies

More suited to what Urban II had intended were five independent armies that formed in 1096 CE. Drawn primarily from France, these forces also included recruits from Flanders, Lorraine, Burgundy, and southern Italy. Following the pope's plan, they intended to converge on Constantinople and then proceed to the Holy Land.

The first (and smallest) of these armies was led by Hugh of Vermandois, brother of Philip I of France. Another French army was commanded by Robert of Flanders, who marched his troops into Italy and then sailed from Bari to the Holy Land. Raymond of Toulouse led the largest contingent, ten thousand men, who marched from Lyon, across the top of Italy, and down the northern shore of the Adriatic Sea. Godfrey of Bouillon traveled through Hungary, where, because his troops were more disciplined than the peasant army, he encountered less resistance from the Hungarian king. The last army was led by Bohemond of Taranto, the eldest son of Robert Guiscard, a longtime enemy of Byzantium. The First Crusade had no overall commander. The leaders of the various contingents had to agree on a course of action. They were fortunate that Bishop Adhemar proved a formidable diplomat and kept them together during their first campaigns. However, he died in 1098 CE, shortly after the siege of Antioch.

In November of 1096 CE, the Christian armies began arriving in Constantinople. The crusaders were not warmly welcomed. After dispatching the rabble army of Peter the Hermit, the city now treated all crusaders with suspicion. Alexius was particularly skeptical of the motives of the leaders. He suspected that they were hoping to conquer Byzantine lands for themselves, and he insisted that each leader swear allegiance to him. The crusaders were unwilling to do so, but the emperor was powerful enough to put pressure on each one in turn. In addition, Alexius required that they should return to him any former Byzantine lands they conquered. Once the oath was sworn, each new vassal was ferried with his army across the **Bosporus** before the next army arrived.

Pope Urban II

The man who eventually became Urban II was born Odo of Lagery in France around 1040 CE. He became prior of the Benedictine monastery at Cluny in 1072 CE, and then he was elected to the office of pope in 1088 CE. During his term as pope, Urban continued the Cluniac reforms that had been introduced by his predecessors. Urban's particular concerns were ending the schism with the Byzantine Christians and reclaiming the Holy Land from the Muslims.

Urban was delighted when the Byzantine emperor Alexius Comnenus appealed to him for help in recovering Anatolia from the Seljuk Turks. In initiating the Holy War, Urban felt that relations between eastern and western Christianity would be strengthened as soldiers fought side by side against the common enemy of their faith and that by serving in the Holy War soldiers would improve their own chances of personal salvation. Urban died in 1099 CE.

Conquering Antioch

In May of 1097 CE, the crusaders began their first coordinated campaign in Anatolia, besieging the Seljuk stronghold of Nicaea. The city surrendered in June (mainly due to astute negotiation by Alexius Comnenus, who, to the disappointment of the crusader leaders, agreed that the city should not be sacked). The city's surrender came not a day too soon for the crusaders, who were suffering from a severe shortage of food. Their plight was exacerbated as the campaign continued because the Turks operated a scorched-earth policy, burning crops and stores as they retreated.

On July 1, 1097 CE, the crusaders won a resounding victory over the Turks at the Battle of Dorylaeum. Although the Christians were outmaneuvered at first, a sudden cavalry charge by heavily armored crusader knights shattered the Turks. The invaders then moved on to the ancient city of Antioch (in northern Syria), which they besieged in October. They managed to enter the city, but they were then trapped by a relief force while the citadel of Antioch held out against them.

Many rank-and-file crusaders were given fresh hope when a priest from southern France claimed to have had a dream in which Saint Andrew showed him the location of the lance used to pierce Christ's side and told him that whoever possessed this relic would be invincible. There was considerable dispute about the meaning of the vision, but the crusaders eventually left the city and defeated the relief force. The emir in the citadel then surrendered, and most of his warriors agreed to be baptized as Christians.

The siege of Antioch, shown here in a fourteenth-century CE manuscript, was a critical standoff of the First Crusade.

After the surrender of Antioch, the crusaders spent the next few months ravaging the surrounding countryside and squabbling over who should control the city. The Byzantine claim to Antioch was forgotten, and many of the crusading nobles wanted to claim it for themselves, following the example of Godfrey of Bouillon's brother, Baldwin, who had seized Edessa and created his own state. Antioch was eventually awarded to Bohemond as a county (a region ruled by a count). The city remained in the hands of his descendants until 1268 CE.

On to Jerusalem

In November of 1098 CE, Raymond of Toulouse led his crusader forces south, and the other leaders, with the exception of Bohemond, followed him. They entered territory controlled not by the Seljuk Turks but by the **Fatimid** rulers of Egypt, who had taken Jerusalem from the Turks in August of 1098 CE. In June of 1099 CE, the exhausted crusader army pitched camp at the gates of Jerusalem. After a solemn pilgrimage to the Jordan River, and after acquiring fresh supplies from a Genoese fleet, the crusaders constructed siege towers and attacked the city. On July 15, they succeeded in taking a section of the city wall and opening a gate. The Fatimid governor surrendered and was given safe conduct out of the city, but the crusader forces then massacred all the Muslim and Jewish inhabitants of Jerusalem. A Fatimid relief force was driven off, and having achieved their goal, many of the crusaders returned home to Europe.

Godfrey of Bouillon was elected to rule Jerusalem and the conquered territories around it. He chose not to be called king because, as he said, he did not want a golden crown when "Christ had worn a thorny crown." Instead, he took the title "Protector of the Holy Sepulchre." Godfrey died after only a year in office, and his brother, Baldwin of Edessa, was chosen to succeed him. Having no objection to a coronation, Baldwin became the first king of Jerusalem.

In the immediate aftermath of the capture of Jerusalem, several crusader states were formed: the county of Edessa in the north, the principality of Antioch, the county of Tripoli, and the kingdom of Jerusalem itself. These crusader states were always precarious. They remained enclaves in Muslim territory and were constantly in danger of attack. The success of the First Crusade was the result not so much of the strength of the Christian armies but of the weakness of the Muslims. The Seljuks had been split into several different states while they were at war with the Fatimids of Egypt. Strong Muslim rulers could easily make inroads, as the Seljuk leader Imad ad-Din Zangi did in 1144 CE, when, from his base in Mosul (a city in modern Iraq), he took the county of Edessa.

The Second Crusade

After Jerusalem was taken by the crusaders in 1099 CE, the kingdom of Jerusalem was able to maintain itself as one of a number of small competing Christian and Muslim states in the region. Its rulers faced a constant manpower shortage, however, because there were insufficient Christian settlers to form the basis of a large feudal-style army. The kingdom's defenses relied heavily on the warrior monks of two orders, the **Knights Templar** and the **Knights Hospitaller**, whose ranks had to be constantly replenished by new recruits from Europe. Thus, when a strong leader emerged to unite the various Muslim states of Syria and northern Iraq, the Christian states were in grave danger.

The leader in question was Imad ad-Din Zangi, the ruler of the territories of Mosul and Aleppo (a city in modern Syria). Under his leadership, the Muslims were able to reconquer Edessa in 1144 CE and then threaten the kingdom of Jerusalem itself.

The crusaders in Jerusalem sent an urgent plea for help to the pope, Eugenius III (ruled 1145–1153 CE), and in 1145 CE, the pope called for a new crusade to relieve the Holy City. King Louis VII of France and Conrad, the Holy Roman emperor, both raised armies and departed for Palestine, passing through Constantinople on the way. As had happened half a century earlier with the First Crusade, the armies, particularly the Germans, were undisciplined and caused havoc as they passed through Byzantine territory.

The armies, understandably, were not popular with the Byzantines by the time they reached Constantinople, and the Byzantine emperor quickly sent them on their way. The German army was ambushed and cut to pieces by Turkish forces near Dorylaeum in 1147 CE. Only a small number of the French crusaders managed to reach Palestine, where they made a strategic error. Instead of attacking the Turks who had conquered Edessa, the crusaders targeted Damascus. The latter, while geographically nearer, was an independent city-state also facing threats from the Turks; it might have been an ally in the crusade.

In July of 1148 CE, the crusaders mounted a wave of assaults on Damascus, but its walls were strong and the attackers were repelled over and over. After only five days of fighting, the crusaders withdrew, and the remnants of their armies returned home to Europe. The fiasco of the **Second Crusade** was over.

Saladin Occupies Jerusalem

Pressure mounted on the kingdom of Jerusalem under Zangi's successor, Nur ad-Din, who developed his realm into a major power. Commanded by the legendary Saladin (ca. 1138–1193 CE), Nur ad-Din's forces conquered Egypt in 1169 CE. After Nur ad-Din's death in 1174 CE, Saladin took over, vowing to recapture Jerusalem for the Muslim faith. Saladin's forces, in control of both Syria and Egypt, almost surrounded the crusader states. Having allowed a truce with Saladin to be broken, Guy de Lusignan, king of Jerusalem (ruled 1186–1194 CE), was crushingly defeated in 1187 CE at the Battle of Hattin, around 20 miles (32 kilometers) west of the Sea of Galilee. In October, Saladin occupied Jerusalem and allowed Christian inhabitants to leave unharmed after paying a ransom.

Saladin retook Jerusalem from the European crusaders in 1187 CE.

The Third Crusade

Pope Gregory VIII called for a **Third Crusade** in October of 1187 CE. The expedition was eventually led by the French king Philip II, the Holy Roman emperor Frederick I, and the English king **Richard I the Lionheart**. They commanded the largest army of crusaders since 1096 CE, but they did not retake Jerusalem. Frederick died before reaching the Holy Land, and his soldiers returned to Germany. Philip and Richard succeeded in securing a number of cities on the Mediterranean, reestablishing a small Latin kingdom (based in the port of Acre) that lasted for a century. Although the Third Crusade failed to achieve its objective, it was more successful than those that followed it.

The Influence of Innocent III

Innocent III was born in 1160 CE to a leading Italian family in Rome. He was well educated and ambitious. Due to family connections, he was made pope in 1198 CE at the age of thirty-seven. He was one of the most worldly and politically minded popes, and during his reign, the papacy achieved its greatest influence over the monarchs of Europe. In some cases, kings actually had to swear fealty to Innocent.

Innocent's dream was to see Jerusalem freed from Muslim control, and in 1202 CE, he inaugurated the Fourth Crusade. Although the expedition ended in failure, the pope did not give up; less than a year before his death, he extracted a promise from the young German emperor, Frederick II, that he would lead another crusade to liberate the Holy City.

The pope's religious fervor also had results closer to home. In 1209 CE, Innocent instigated a crusade against the Albigensians in southern France, declaring that heresy was "treason against God" and that it must be rooted out at all costs. Innocent did not live to see the outcome of this crusade; he died in 1216 CE.

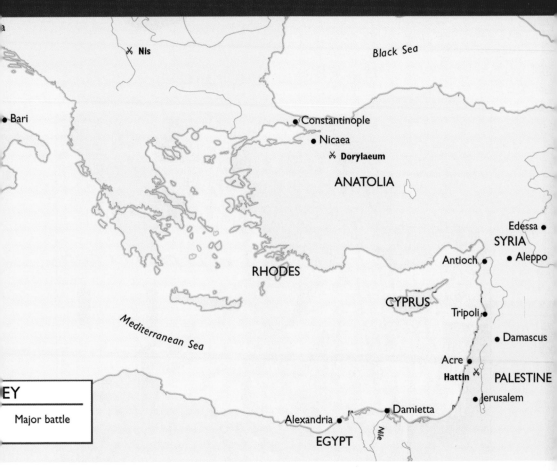

Nis ✗

Black Sea

• Bari

• Constantinople

• Nicaea

✗ Dorylaeum

ANATOLIA

Edessa •

SYRIA

Antioch • • Aleppo

RHODES

CYPRUS

Tripoli •

• Damascus

Mediterranean Sea

Acre •

Hattin ✗ PALESTINE

EY

Major battle

• Jerusalem

Alexandria • • Damietta

EGYPT

Nile

The Sack of Constantinople

Hoping to recapture the Holy City, the new pope, Innocent III (see sidebar, page 42), called for the Fourth Crusade in 1198 CE. The venture got off to a bad start. In 1202 CE, the crusaders joined with Venetian forces who wanted to recapture Zara (modern Zadar, Croatia) from the Hungarians. When the pope heard of the diversion, he was furious and excommunicated the whole expedition. The crusaders then joined forces with a claimant to the Byzantine throne and seized Constantinople on his behalf. However, once the emperor had been reinstated, he refused to pay for their services. The crusaders then considered themselves justified in plundering the city, which they did with appalling brutality.

The Albigensian Heresy

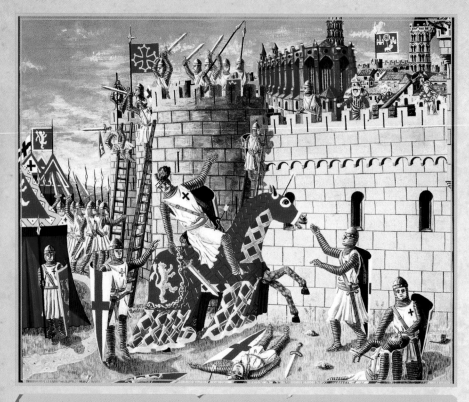

This thirteenth-century CE manuscript depicts the death of Simon de Montfort the Elder at the Battle of Toulouse, part of the Albigensian Crusade.

The major crusade fought in Europe was proclaimed in 1209 CE by Pope Innocent III against the Albigenses, a heretical sect based in Carcassonne and the surrounding region of Languedoc in southern France.

The Albigenses were **Cathars**, a group that held there was a god of good competing with a separate god of evil. The god of goodness and light was identified with Jesus Christ and the God in the New Testament of the Bible. The god of evil and darkness was identified with the devil and the God in the Old Testament. The Cathars believed in reincarnation and that the only way to escape being reborn as a person or an animal was to lead a good life on earth; such a life would be rewarded with a spiritual existence after death.

Cathars lived either as simple believers (who led ordinary lives) or as perfects (ascetics). The perfects were believed to be able to commune with God in prayer; they were strict vegetarians and were not allowed possessions or sexual relations. Simple believers could become perfects through a rite called consolamentum (consolation), a "laying on of hands" that was frequently administered just before death.

The Albigensian heresy had a political aspect. The Cathars regarded the Roman Catholic Church, with all its corruption, wealth, and interest in material power, as the agent of the devil. In the first period of the crusade against the Albigenses, Simon de Montfort the Elder (ca. 1165–1218 CE) led an army of around ten thousand knights from France and Burgundy to combat the heretical forces under the count of Toulouse, whose ancestor, Raymond of Toulouse, had led the largest contingent on the First Crusade.

The first phase of the Albigensian Crusade was ended in 1229 CE by the Treaty of Paris. The heresy remained, however, and soon provoked a second period of hostilities, which lasted until around 1271 CE. Captured heretics were handed over to the Inquisition, which tortured them in an effort to force them to renounce their beliefs. Many, however, preferred death to dishonor. On one occasion, in 1244 CE, some two hundred Cathars were burned alive on a great pyre in the town of Montségur.

Because the property of the Cathars and their sympathizers was confiscated, the Albigensian Crusade brought a large territory in southern France under the control of the French crown. The Albigensian heresy was not fully crushed until the fourteenth century CE.

After sacking Constantinople, the crusaders installed their own emperor, Count Baldwin of Flanders, whose coronation as Baldwin I in May of 1204 CE initiated a period of Latin rule over Byzantium. In 1228 CE, Baldwin II inherited the throne at the age of eleven. John of Brienne, a former king of Jerusalem, took over as regent, and Baldwin spent much of his adult life in Europe, trying to gather an army to recover the parts of his empire that had been seized by the Bulgarians and Greeks. Latin rule ended in 1261 CE, when Baldwin lost Constantinople to the Byzantine emperor Michael VIII.

Crusaders in Egypt

Rather than targeting Jerusalem, the **Fifth Crusade** was directed toward Egypt. This was one of the least successful crusades. In 1219 CE, the Christian warriors captured the Egyptian port of Damietta, but the reinforcements that they needed and expected never materialized. The crusaders failed to take Cairo and were forced to hand Damietta back in 1221 CE. After that loss, the crusaders retreated to Europe.

Additional Crusades

Frederick II had vowed in 1215 CE and again in 1220 CE that he would lead a crusade to the Holy Land, and Pope Gregory IX was anxious to make the emperor keep his promise. Frederick finally set sail in 1227 CE, but an epidemic forced him to return to port. The pope promptly excommunicated the emperor. A year later, Frederick sailed to Egypt and negotiated with the Egyptian sultan Al Kamil, who surrendered Jerusalem to the emperor in 1229 CE and signed a ten-year peace treaty.

Jerusalem again proved difficult to defend, and in 1244 CE, the city fell to Turkish and Egyptian forces. In Europe, there was a flurry of interest in a crusade to recapture the Holy City. Louis IX of France spent years planning a campaign before he sailed from Cyprus and captured Damietta in June of 1249 CE. However, his attempt on Cairo the following spring was defeated when the Egyptians opened reservoir sluice gates along the Nile River, trapping the French army and forcing Louis to surrender in April of 1250 CE. The king paid a ransom to secure his own release and was forced to hand back Damietta. He then sailed for Palestine, where he spent four years helping to improve the defenses of the Latin kingdom.

Back in France, Louis tried in 1270 CE to mobilize support for another crusade against the city of Tunis. The French nobility was unsupportive, but Louis carried on regardless and died in Tunisia the same year.

The remaining crusader strongholds in western Asia fell one by one to the new rulers of Egypt—the **Mamluk** dynasty. Acre succumbed in May of 1291 CE, and its Christian occupiers fled first to Cyprus and then to Rhodes. Although the Europeans made further sporadic attempts to regain lost territory—including a Cyprus-based attack on Alexandria, Egypt, in 1365 CE—the crusades had run their course.

The fifteenth and sixteenth centuries CE saw renewed papal calls for further crusades, this time to stem the incursion of the Ottoman Turks into western Europe. These efforts were largely defensive, however. They were far removed from the brash, conquest-oriented rallying cries that had European noblemen and peasants alike up in arms in the previous centuries.

This detail from the Bayeux Tapestry depicts a Norman ship on its way to England. The Normans descended from Danish Vikings.

CHAPTER FOUR

The Spread of the Vikings

The Vikings—also known as the Norsemen—were pagans from the northern European region of Scandinavia. At home in present-day Denmark, Norway, and Sweden, their longships and expert navigational skills allowed them to explore and sometimes colonize large stretches of the Northern Hemisphere, ranging from the Black Sea all the way to the eastern shores of North America. Fearsome raiders, they sailed the seas and rivers of Europe, plundering villages and monasteries, taking towns, creating their own principalities, and even holding whole countries for ransom. They were a force to be reckoned with from the eighth to the eleventh centuries CE.

The Vikings were not just warriors, however. They were also farmers, fishermen, and merchants, able to buy to and sell in distant countries. They traded in furs, precious metals, and foodstuffs such as dried herring. Above all, though, they traded in slaves. Indeed, the very name of the Slav peoples of eastern Europe comes from the word slave, because so many Slavs were captured and sold into slavery by the Vikings.

The Conquest of England

Some Vikings set out by sea from their homelands with the specific intention of raiding and plundering. Their principal targets were Christian communities in England and elsewhere that had completely undefended monasteries laden with wealth.

In June of 793 CE, a party of Vikings attacked and sacked the monastery of Lindisfarne, an island off the northeastern coast of England. The monks were either killed or taken prisoner to be sold as slaves; the monastery was destroyed, and everything of value was looted. The event sent shockwaves through the Christian world. The Lindisfarne raid was the first of many similar attacks on monasteries and isolated communities as the Viking marauders targeted the islands around Scotland and Ireland.

By the second half of the ninth century CE, Viking ships were regularly plundering the eastern and southern coasts of England, where they encountered little effective resistance. England at that time was divided into four main kingdoms—Northumbria in the north, East Anglia in the east, Mercia in the midlands, and Wessex in the south. The kingdoms were rivals and often at war with each other; united opposition to the common enemy was therefore impractical. When the Viking raiders appeared, the local inhabitants simply fled.

In 865 CE, three Viking brothers—Halfdan, Ivar the Boneless, and Ubbi—landed an armed force in East Anglia and marched north to **Eboracum** (modern York). They captured the ancient Roman city, which was then the capital of Northumbria, and turned it into a mighty fortress of their own.

The Viking force in Eboracum became known as the Great Army. It fought off two Northumbrian lords and secured the whole of Northumbria. Ivar then headed south to East Anglia, where he defeated and killed the local king. The Vikings, in possession of two of the English kingdoms, also made inroads into Mercia. They were then content to settle for what they had won, and most of them reverted to their original occupation as farmers.

In 871 CE, another Viking leader, Guthrum, attacked Wessex. The new king of Wessex, **Alfred the Great** (ruled 871– 899 CE), made a determined stand against the invaders. Hostilities continued for several years, and then, around 878 CE, the two sides signed a treaty that recognized the right of the Vikings to settle in northeastern England. Because most of the Vikings who took part in the invasion were Danes, the area became known as the **Danelaw**. Under the terms of the treaty, Guthrum also agreed to be baptized as a Christian.

The struggle between the Vikings and the English was far from over, however. Despite Alfred's efforts to protect Wessex, the Vikings remained entrenched in much of northern and eastern England, and during the tenth and early eleventh centuries CE, Scandinavian campaigns to capture Wessex intensified. In 1013 CE, Sweyn Forkbeard (the overlord of Norway, Sweden, and Denmark) arrived in northern England with a great army, and the established inhabitants of the Danelaw swore allegiance to him. Marching southward, Forkbeard's forces so intimidated the English that many abandoned the Wessex king, Aethelred the Unready (ruled 978–1016 CE), and joined forces with the Scandinavians. Aethelred fled to Normandy, and Forkbeard claimed the whole of England as his own. Forkbeard's triumph was short-lived, however; he died suddenly only a few weeks later, leaving his new kingdom to his son, **Cnut** (or Canute).

This stained glass window at Canterbury Cathedral depicts King Cnut.

The transfer of power from Sweyn Forkbeard to Cnut was not smooth. Aethelred returned from exile with a new army, and Cnut had to fight for his inheritance. However, Aethelred and his son Edmund Ironside both died in 1016 CE, and Cnut became undisputed king of the whole of England, which he ruled until his death in 1035 CE. Cnut held sway over a vast empire that consisted of England, Norway, Denmark, and some of what is now Sweden.

French Incursions

At the beginning of the ninth century CE, the emperor Charlemagne (ruled 800–814 CE) was the most powerful monarch in Europe, presiding over a vast Carolingian Empire that included much of France, Germany, the Netherlands, and northern Italy. However, his lands were not immune to the northern raiders. In 810 CE, some two hundred Danish longships raided the coast of Frisia and demanded tribute. In the 840s CE, the Danes sacked the Frankish towns of Rouen, Chartres, and Tours; by the middle of the ninth century CE, extensive areas of France were effectively in Danish hands. In late 885 CE, an army of thirty thousand Danes, carried in seven hundred longships, sailed up the Seine River and laid siege to Paris. However, they failed to capture the city. After weeks of fighting and serious casualties on both sides, the Frankish king, Charles the Fat (ruled 876–888 CE), arrived with troops and made a deal with the Danes. In return for a sum of money and free passage out of the area, the Danes agreed to lift the siege, sail farther inland, and help Charles to put down an uprising by the people of Burgundy.

Following their repeated raids into northern France, the Danish Vikings eventually settled permanently in the region. At the beginning of the tenth century CE, their leader, Rollo, agreed to a treaty with the Frankish king, Charles the Simple (ruled 893–922 CE). Rollo swore allegiance to Charles and set about defending the territory then known as Neustria (modern Normandy) on his behalf. Rollo became duke of Normandy in 911 CE, and he agreed to become a Christian. His warriors were all granted land and settled down into a feudal society. The Normans then entered an era of expansionism that brought them, in 1066 CE, the throne of England and, later, their own state in southern Italy and Sicily. Norman knights also played an important role in the First Crusade.

To Constantinople and Beyond

Unlike the Danish and Norwegian Vikings, who sailed southward and westward, the Swedish Vikings directed their expeditions eastward across the Baltic Sea into lands that gave them access to the rivers of eastern Europe. From the early ninth century CE, Swedish Vikings made regular raids across the region, exacting tributes from the Slavic nobles and enslaving large numbers of ordinary people. They then established a trade route from their homelands, across eastern Europe, and south into the Byzantine, Arab, and Turkish states of the eastern Mediterranean and western Asia. The prosperity of this commercial artery is evidenced by the discovery, in 2006 CE, of more than one thousand Arab silver coins buried on the Swedish island of Gotland in the Baltic Sea.

The Swedish traders and raiders gradually took over the Slavic tribes of the eastern Baltic coast. A semi-legendary leader named Rurik established himself at **Novgorod** (a city in modern Russia). Two other Viking leaders, Askold and Dir, pressed on along the Dnieper River to **Kiev**, almost 600 miles (960 km) to the south.

Kiev later became a vital link on the prosperous trade route between Scandinavia and Constantinople. In 860 CE, a Viking force of two hundred longships completed a foray along the whole length of the Dnieper River and reached Constantinople itself. Realizing immediately that they would be unable to take the city, the Vikings instead plundered the surrounding villages and monasteries, slaughtering the inhabitants without mercy. They sailed away laden with booty.

The leaders of that expedition were the rulers of Kiev, Askold and Dir. Oleg, who had gained power in Novgorod after Rurik's death, quickly decided that the continued division of power in the region was unsatisfactory. Oleg invited Askold and Dir to a meeting, claiming that he wanted to make joint plans for the future, but when they arrived, he had them both murdered. Oleg became supreme ruler of the new state, known as Kievan Rus.

According to a twelfth-century CE account, another Viking expedition set out for Constantinople around 907 CE. It was a substantial force of eighty thousand men in two thousand ships, under the command of Oleg. Already involved in a war with the Bulgars in the Balkans, the Byzantine emperor agreed to talk terms with the Vikings. He paid a large tribute and, more important, ratified a trade agreement that allowed the Vikings to enter the city for the purpose of trade.

Oleg now controlled an immensely lucrative trade route, from Constantinople to the Baltic Sea, but he was still not satisfied. The

Vikings penetrated the lands of the Khazars, the region between the Black Sea and the Caspian Sea. In return for half of the proceeds, the Khazars agreed to allow the Vikings to sail up their rivers on the way to plunder Arab territories beyond the Caspian Sea. However, the Khazars underestimated the ferocity of the Viking raids.

When the Khazars heard how the Vikings had ravaged the countryside, burning towns and massacring the inhabitants, they assembled an army and confronted the Vikings on their return. In the ensuing battle, the Viking leader (probably Oleg) was killed.

Oleg's successor, Igor, was murdered in 945 CE by Derevlian Slavs (from whom he had demanded very high taxes), but his widow, Olga, proved to be a formidable leader. Ruling at first as regent for her young son, Svyatoslav, she ruthlessly eliminated the Derevlian opposition. Even after Svyatoslav took over, Olga remained the power behind the throne for the next twenty-four years.

Svyatoslav wanted to extend his kingdom even farther. If he could conquer territory as far as the Volga River, he reasoned, he would then control all the trade routes between the Baltic Sea and the Caspian Sea. In the 960s CE, Svyatoslav marched his army to the Khazar capital of Itl, on the banks of the Volga River. He destroyed the city and then subdued much of the lower Danube region, thereby tripling the size of his dominions. However, during his long absence from Kiev, the city had been besieged by the **Pechenegs**, a warrior people from central Asia, so he was forced to hurry home to save his mother and his children.

Having forced the Pechenegs to withdraw, Svyatoslav appointed his three sons as regents and marched on Constantinople. However, a defeat in 971 CE forced him to make peace with the Byzantine Empire. On the return journey to Kiev in 972 CE, Svyatoslav and his men were ambushed by the Pechenegs and massacred.

Svyatoslav's son **Vladimir the Great** was keen to maintain good relations with Constantinople. In 988 CE, the Byzantine emperor Basil II offered his sister Anna's hand in marriage to Vladimir—on condition that Vladimir convert to Christianity. Because Anna would bring lands in the Crimea as her dowry and the marriage would create an alliance with Constantinople, Vladimir accepted. His baptism was a momentous occasion in the history of Russia. In the years that followed, many of his subjects abandoned their old pagan gods and embraced the new faith. The spread of Orthodox Christianity in Russia meant that the country would forever be under the influence of the eastern church.

Vikings in Iceland

From the eighth century CE, the Norwegian Vikings had used the Shetland Islands (between Norway and Scotland) as a convenient base from which to launch attacks on the coastal settlements of Britain. In the ninth century CE, Viking ships appeared near the Faroe Islands, 200 miles (320 km) north of the Shetlands, and before long, the islands were colonized by Vikings, driving out the Irish monks who had previously inhabited them.

The Viking Longship

The success of the Viking raids depended on their longships, which were fast, sturdily built warships. A typical longship was around 60–80 feet (18–24 meters) from stem to stern, a narrow boat constructed from overlapping oak planks. It had a shallow keel, which allowed it to navigate rivers, and it was powered by sail and oars.

There were around thirty oarsmen on each side of a ship. Rowing together, they could propel the vessel in calm weather conditions, while a large, rectangular cloth sail enabled the ship to sail in favorable breezes at up to 10 knots (11.5 miles per hour; 18.5 kilometers per hour). At that speed, the Vikings could cross from Norway to England in twenty-four hours.

Viking longships were distinguished, above all, by their fearsome dragon's head prows.

On the prow of each warship was a carved dragon's head, the appearance of which was calculated to inspire fear in all who saw it. The longship's sails were often brightly colored to draw attention to the fleet. When sailing on a hostile raid, the warriors often hung their shields along the outside of the ship's hull.

The Vikings were excellent navigators, which enabled them to make their hair-raising crossings of the Atlantic Ocean. They navigated by the sun and stars, and they may have had help from a mysterious sunstone, a crystal that polarized light. Despite the fact that their vessels were oceangoing, they were also light enough to be hauled overland when necessary, such as, for example, on un-navigable stretches of the Dnieper River during the advance to Kiev in the ninth century CE. The Vikings placed their ships on tree trunks, which were used as rollers.

In the middle of the ninth century CE, several Viking sailors were blown off course, ending up 600 miles (960 km) west of Norway, on a large and apparently uninhabited island. One of the seafarers, Raven Floki, spent the summer there, living on salmon and seal. The favorable weather conditions gave Floki and his companions a false sense of security; they were quite unprepared for the severity of the winter that followed, and when they managed to make it back to Norway, they gave the island its discouraging name—Iceland.

Despite that unpromising start, many other Vikings followed in Floki's footsteps and, better prepared than he had been, successfully settled the island. There was plenty of land suitable for farming, an abundance of fish, and vast forests to yield timber for building. Within sixty years, it is estimated that the population of Iceland exceeded ten thousand.

In the late ninth century CE, a warrior named Harald Finehair (ruled 860–930 CE) overcame all his rivals and became the first king of Norway. The emergence of a monarchy prompted many Norwegians to abandon their homes and seek new lands in which they could live without having to obey a ruler they had never wanted.

By 930 CE, so many Norwegian settlers had arrived in Iceland that there was little workable land left for the taking. As even more and more colonists continued to pour in, quarrels arose, and it became necessary to form some sort of government. A republic was set up, governed by a parliament known as the Althing, which met once a year at midsummer. Regional bodies, called Things, met more often, and every freeman was eligible to attend and speak at them. The Thing had great powers. It could make laws, act as a law court, and even make the decision to go to war.

Around the beginning of the eleventh century CE, Iceland became Christianized. By that time, most European countries, including those of Scandinavia, were already Christian, and pressure was brought to bear on the Icelanders to conform. At a meeting of the Althing, it was decided to adopt Christianity as the community's official religion, although pagan practices were still allowed. The compromise seemed to satisfy everyone, and the whole population was baptized en masse.

Exploring Greenland

After 930 CE, when most of the best land in Iceland had been taken, Viking settlers started looking even farther afield. From the most westerly point of Iceland, it was sometimes possible to catch a glimpse of a coast to the west. At one point, a sailor named Gunnbjörn Ulfsson was swept past Iceland during a violent storm and made landfall on some unprepossessing rocks that became known as Gunnbjörn's Skerries. Ulfsson and other Viking mariners soon became convinced that there was land even farther to the west.

The first Scandinavian to venture intentionally into the unknown waters off the west coast of Iceland was an Icelandic farmer named Erik the Red. His decision to travel was forced on him by his local Thing, which, in 982 CE, banished him for three years for murdering the son of one of his neighbors. With nowhere else to go, Erik fitted out a ship and embarked on a desperate journey in search of land that no one knew existed. After four days' sailing, he and his crew sighted a forbidding coastline of towering cliffs. Turning southward, they sailed on until they found a safe haven on the coast. They disembarked at the southern tip of what appeared to be a very large island. There were green meadows for crops and grazing, and Erik and his party settled there for three years. During that time, they explored the territory, and although the northern part of it (which was above the Arctic Circle) was icy and uninhabitable, the southern part (which was warmed by the Gulf Stream) offered plenty of cultivatable land. At the end of his enforced exile, Erik the Red returned to Iceland with enthusiastic reports of this new region, ripe for the taking, which he optimistically named Greenland.

In 986 CE, Erik the Red led a fleet carrying settlers and their livestock in a sortie to set up a colony on Greenland. Of the twenty-five ships that set out, only fourteen made landfall on Greenland; the others were lost in storms and ice floes along the way. Around 450 surviving members of the expedition set up a colony on the west coast, where the deep fjords reminded them of their native Norway. Although life was hard, the settlers prospered, and a Viking community remained in Greenland for almost five hundred years.

Viking Religion and Life

The Vikings were descendants of Germanic tribes who migrated to northern Europe around 2000 BCE. They eventually settled in Scandinavia—present-day Norway, Sweden, and Denmark—where they became farmers and traders. They were a pagan people, worshipping the Nordic gods—whose king was Odin, the god of war and death. Another important god was Thor, the god of thunder and lightning. The Norse myths are powerful stories that were passed orally from generation to generation until the twelfth century CE, when they were first written down by scribes in Iceland.

This bronze statuette of the Viking god Thor, holding his hammer, was found in Iceland.

Most Vikings were freemen. They either tilled the land (growing crops such as grain, vegetables, and fruit, and keeping animals such as goats, cattle, and sheep) or were craftsmen and merchants. Below these freemen were slaves, many of whom had been captured during raids. Slaves worked as laborers on the farms and manned the oars on the longships. They had a life of unremitting hardship, and they had no rights. At the top of society were the nobles and chieftains, each of whom might command the services of freemen in the numerous internal struggles for land or on pirate voyages to seize loot or land abroad.

The Vikings lived in villages of single-story wooden huts that had roofs of turf but no windows. At the center of some villages, there was a larger longhouse in which the chieftain lived with his family, farmworkers, and animals. The most powerful chieftains controlled very large regions. They often went to war with rival leaders to eliminate competition and increase their own landholdings.

Leif Eriksson in the New World

Erik the Red's second son, **Leif Eriksson** (ca. 970–1020 CE), inherited his father's adventurous spirit. As a boy, he had heard the tale of an Icelander named Bjarni Herjolfsson, who, having been blown off course while attempting to sail to Greenland, sighted an unexplored land far to the west. Refusing to make landfall on this strange coastline, which he noted was well forested, Bjarni turned and sailed east for four days before reaching his intended destination, the coast of Greenland.

The archaeological site at L'Anse aux Meadows in Newfoundland features reconstructions of Viking turf houses.

Around 1000 CE, Eriksson bought Bjarni's ship and planned an expedition to discover and explore the unknown country. Setting sail from Greenland, Eriksson followed the course of Bjarni's homeward voyage and, after several days, made landfall at a place that is thought to have been Baffin Island in modern Canada. He named his discovery Helluland (the land of flat stones). Continuing south, Eriksson found a densely wooded stretch of coastline, which he named Markland (forest land)—and which may have been Labrador. After two further days at sea, the expedition sighted land for a third time and decided to go ashore for the winter. The place, which Eriksson named Vinland, is now known as Newfoundland. There, in 1960 CE, archaeologists unearthed an extensive Viking settlement that may have been Eriksson's encampment. Now fully excavated, the site at L'Anse aux Meadows consists of turf houses (that would have accommodated around ninety people), a smithy, and facilities for repairing ships. It is possible that the Vikings explored even farther to the south.

Eriksson returned to Greenland and reported that he had found a fertile, well-endowed land. Three more Viking voyages were made to Vinland, but the settlers abandoned their attempts to establish a colony in the face of hostility from the indigenous Native Americans.

While the Vikings may have given up on their plans to settle North America, it is thought that they didn't completely turn their backs on the continent. Indeed, many scholars believe that Viking sailors continued to make westward excursions for several centuries in search of new sources of lumber, an important but scarce commodity in northern Europe. Whether or not this is the case, it is an accepted—though often overlooked—fact that Leif Eriksson explored the New World some five hundred years before Christopher Columbus famously "discovered" it.

Saint Basil's Cathedral in Moscow was built in the sixteenth century CE, during the reign of Ivan the Terrible.

CHAPTER FIVE

The Birth of Russia

Civilization began developing in Russia during the sixth century CE. Initially, the country's power was concentrated in the city of Kiev, located in present-day Ukraine. Over time, **Moscow** rose in prominence. It became Russia's capital in the fifteenth century CE.

While the history of every state is critically affected by its geography, there is perhaps no country in which the landscape and topography have had as great an influence on human events as they have had in Russia. Russia's most striking characteristic is, of course, its great size, but also important has been its lack of natural land boundaries. In the south of the country, the enormous open steppes provided an easy invasion route for nomadic, mounted tribesmen from central Asia. Similarly, in the west, the absence of a clearly defined natural frontier encouraged incursions from inhabitants of the plains of Europe. The heart of Russia, however, was sharply defined by its principal rivers, especially the Dnieper, the Don, and the Volga, which all flow from north to south and offer great potential for trade. The story of medieval Russia may be divided into four phases: the creation of a state based on river-borne trading opportunities; the breakup of that state as trade declined and pressure from the steppe nomads became irresistible; the creation of a new state that was independent from those nomads; and that new state dealing with threats from its western neighbors.

At some time before the fourth century CE, Slavic peoples migrated from the Caucasus to the vast plains between the Black Sea and the Arctic Ocean to settle the area that became known as Russia. The Slavs were mainly hunters and traders. They used the rivers in the region to transport goods between the Baltic Sea and the Black Sea. As commercial activity developed, trading posts were established along the rivers. One of those trading posts was Novgorod, on the Volkhov River, and another was Kiev (Kyiv) on the Dnieper River. By the middle of the sixth century CE, Kiev was firmly established as the most important city in the region. The early inhabitants of Russia had to deal with steppe peoples such as the Avars and, later, the Khazars, who founded a powerful empire based in the lower Volga region.

The first great Russian state was created by the Varangians (Scandinavian Vikings from the area that is now Sweden), who traded and raided deep into Russia along the rivers. The Varangians were ruled by princes, one of whom was named Rurik.

Rurik, seen here in a Novgorod monument, is often cited as the founder of the Russian Empire.

In the ninth century CE, Rurik established himself in Novgorod and united the tribes of northern Russia. Many historians regard Rurik as the founder of the Russian Empire, and it is certain that he ushered in a period of expansion, during which the Slavic peoples migrated north, replacing or assimilating the indigenous populations.

Varangians led by Askold and Dir penetrated farther south along the Dnieper River, reaching Kiev and, finally, Constantinople, which they attacked in 860 CE. In 879 CE, Rurik was succeeded by his son, Igor. Igor was still a child, so Oleg was appointed regent. In 882 CE, Oleg had the rulers of Kiev (Askold and Dir) assassinated and made Kiev the capital of the first significant Russian state, Kievan Rus. Around 907 CE, Oleg made a treaty with the Byzantine Empire that allowed Kievan Rus to control and profit from all the trade between the Baltic Sea and Constantinople.

Governing Kievan Rus

The political history of Kiev begins with Oleg's conquest of the city in 882 CE. It is not clear, however, when the Kiev Empire ceased to exist. Some historians maintain that the end of the empire coincided with the death of Yaroslav the Wise in 1054 CE, while others assert that Vladimir Monomachus (ruled 1113–1125 CE) was the last ruler. Alternatively, the last Kievan emperor may have been Mstislav (ruled 1125–1132 CE A few historians see the conquest of Kiev by Andrew Bogolyubsky in 1169 CE as the end of the empire. The most convenient date is probably 1240 CE, when Kiev was destroyed by the **Mongols**.

The most important political institutions in Kievan Rus were the office of prince, the *duma* (council of boyars), and the *veche* (city council). The prince of Kiev held a very special position. From the early twelfth century CE, he was called the grand prince. He commanded the army, controlled the administration of justice, and was the head of government. In times of war, the grand prince called first on his *druzhina* (his personal liegemen). In extreme cases, he could order a general mobilization of all his subjects.

Kievan Rus was very well organized, especially where trade and finance were concerned, and the penalties that were imposed by the legal system tended to be fines rather than physical punishments. The government raised finances by taxing fireplaces and plowshares and by levying duties on trade.

The duma worked in consultation with the grand prince but could not overrule him. The veche, however, which convened in the marketplace, had much greater powers. Its decisions in emergencies and in conflicts between members of the ruling families appear to have been highly influential and often binding. The effectiveness of the Kievan veche inspired the creation of similar bodies in other Russian cities, notably Novgorod, which had its own veche until it was taken over by Moscow.

Oleg died soon after signing that treaty. He was succeeded by Igor, who ruled for three decades and greatly expanded the empire. On Igor's death in 945 CE, the throne passed to his widow, Olga. Olga further extended Kievan influence. Meanwhile, a new external threat had emerged—the Pechenegs, a warlike, seminomadic people from the southern steppes.

In 964 CE, Olga's son, Svyatoslav, came of age and inherited the throne. By the time Svyatoslav was ambushed and killed by Pechenegs in 972 CE, he had developed his kingdom into a large empire that included much of modern Ukraine. After Svyatoslav's death, his three sons fought each other for the throne. Eventually, the youngest son, Vladimir, became the undisputed ruler of Kievan Rus.

Conversion to Christianity

Vladimir the Great (Vladimir I; ruled 980–1015 CE) is widely regarded as the architect of the Kievan state. He consolidated his empire, which now extended from Ukraine to the Baltic Sea, and strengthened its borders so that his armies were better equipped to repel raids by the steppe nomads.

The baptism of Vladimir the Great, shown in this fifteenth-century CE manuscript, marked the beginning of Orthodox Christianity in Russia.

Vladimir was also responsible for converting the people of Kievan Rus to Orthodox Christianity. This decision was primarily political rather than spiritually motivated. Vladimir himself was a pagan; he was more interested in overcoming his enemies and in the pursuit of his own pleasures than in religious matters. However, in 988 CE, the Byzantine emperor Basil II, to express his gratitude for Kievan help in suppressing a rebellion, offered his sister Anna's hand in marriage to Vladimir. A condition of the marriage was that Vladimir should convert to his bride's religion, Orthodox Christianity. Because Anna's dowry included rich and extensive Byzantine lands, Vladimir was happy to agree.

Once Vladimir had been baptized, he made Orthodox Christianity the official religion of Kievan Rus. From that time onward, the Orthodox Church played a major role in the development of Russian society. One lasting consequence of the conversion was the adoption in Russia of the Cyrillic alphabet, which was very different from the Roman alphabet used in most of Europe.

On the death of Vladimir in 1015 CE, the throne was seized by his eldest son, Svyatopolk the Accursed, who lost no time in killing two of his brothers. Another brother, Yaroslav, the regent of Novgorod, then enlisted the aid of Scandinavian mercenaries to depose Svyatopolk in 1019 CE

By 1036 CE, Yaroslav had created a great Russian empire that stretched from the Black Sea to the Gulf of Finland. Unlike most of his predecessors, Yaroslav was interested in art and culture. He collected manuscripts of all kinds, and he commissioned scholars to translate Greek texts into Russian. He also built churches and monasteries and started to codify the law, an initiative that formed the basis of the legal code known as Russian Justice.

Yaroslav tried to establish a system of inheritance to avoid the internecine struggles that had been the norm following the deaths of previous grand princes of Kiev. However, his efforts were to no avail. After his own death in 1054 CE, most of Vladimir's numerous grandsons inherited lands and acquired interests in conflict with each other. A profusion of warring city-states developed, most of them ruled by vying members of the royal house of Rurik.

The Waning of Kiev

During the second half of the eleventh century CE, disputes between the competing city-states became more acrimonious and increasingly involved the nomadic peoples in the south of the country. The conflicts weakened Kievan Rus, which lost much of its former cohesion and was sometimes in danger of disintegrating. Yaroslav's grandson, Vladimir Monomachus (ruled 1113–1125 CE), tried to restore order, but his efforts were never fully successful.

An important factor in Kiev's decline was the increasingly difficult trading conditions. Kiev was badly affected when soldiers of the Fourth Crusade sacked Constantinople in 1204 CE. Many citizens of Kiev left for Novgorod, which was increasingly looking west to the Baltic Sea for trade; indeed, in the thirteenth century CE, the Hanseatic League of northern German cities used Novgorod as its base in Russia. Important western regions of the Kievan state, such as Galicia and Volhynia, established independent links with Hungary and Poland, while central authority was also challenged by the boyars (landed nobility). It was in this severely weakened condition that the Kievan state was forced to face a new adversary that threatened its very existence.

The Golden Horde

The new threat to Kiev came from the Mongol army of **Genghis Khan** (1162–1227 CE), which marauded westward from central Asia. The first Mongol incursion into Russia came from the Caucasus and was led by two sons of Genghis. The Mongols later reached the Crimea, and at the mouth of the Dnieper River, they defeated an alliance of Kievan forces and the Polovtsi (a local steppe people). After their victory, the Mongols were recalled to take part in an invasion of China. In 1237 CE, however, they returned. Batu Khan, grandson of Genghis, led Mongol forces in an invasion that destroyed the major Russian cities in the Vladimir-Suzdal region. Batu Khan sacked Kiev in 1240 CE, and Alexander Nevsky saved the city of Novgorod only by the payment of a substantial ransom.

The Mongols then rode westward again, defeating Christian armies in Germany and Hungary. Their advance was halted in 1241 CE, when

Eastern European States

Russia's history during the medieval period was closely entwined with that of three states to its west—Hungary, Poland, and Lithuania. The borders among all four of them ebbed and flowed as power shifted in the region. Hungary, for example, became dominant in western parts of the Kievan realm during the latter's decline in the twelfth century CE, while the rivalry between Russia and Poland was not finally settled until the latter was partitioned in the eighteenth century CE.

All four states suffered severely during the Mongol domination of the southern European steppes, and they all fought against the **Teutonic Knights** at various times in the fourteenth and fifteenth centuries CE. For a while, Poland was united with Hungary, but from 1386 CE, Poland and Lithuania were brought together to form the largest state in Europe under the ruling Jagiellon dynasty.

Poland and Hungary converted to Catholicism early in the Middle Ages, and as a result, their cultural development was quite different from that of Orthodox Russia. Lithuania was a pagan culture until 1386 CE, when the grand duke converted to Catholicism in order to become king of Poland (Wladyslaw II).

Hungary was a major power in the fourteenth and fifteenth centuries CE. Under King Matthias Corvinus (ruled 1458–1490 CE), the nation fought successful campaigns against the Ottoman Turks, who were encroaching north from the Balkan Peninsula, and against the Holy Roman emperor Frederick III. In 1485 CE, Corvinus took Vienna and annexed large areas of what is now Austria. The power politics of eastern Europe during this period were complex. Russian rulers frequently allied with the Ottomans and the steppe nomads against the Catholic states of Poland and Hungary.

they learned of the death of Genghis Khan's heir, Ogotai. On hearing the news, they returned, as they were bound to do under their laws, to Mongolia to settle the succession.

For the next two hundred years, Russian political life was dominated by the authority of the Mongol state in the steppes. Effectively, southern Russia became part of what was called the Empire of the **Golden Horde**. The Mongols made their capital at Sarai, and it was to that city on the lower Volga River that all the Russian principalities had to send tributes to the khans of the Golden Horde. In Sarai, the Russian principalities were represented by the grand prince of Russia, who had to travel to the city to perform obeisance to a representative of the Golden Horde. In addition, Russian military contingents were occasionally required to serve in Mongol forces.

In 1380 CE , the Russians scored a significant victory over the Mongols when Dmitry Donskoy, the grand duke of Moscow, defeated the forces of the Golden Horde at the Battle of Kulikovo on the Don River. However, a resurgent Golden Horde counterattacked and captured Moscow in 1382 CE.

The Rise of Moscow

Although the khans of the Golden Horde demanded tribute and obeisance, they did not interfere in the day-to-day activities of the Russian principalities. Novgorod, for example, thrived as a trading city. It developed its own unique governing system, based on the rule of several important trading families, tempered by the importance of the division of the town into "fifths" and the existence of a veche (town council). Other important centers included the cities of Pskov and Tver.

However, it was Moscow that gradually became both the heart and the strongest arm of the new Russian state. The first of the great dukes of Moscow was Daniel Nevsky, who inherited the town from his father, Alexander Nevsky, in 1263 CE. Daniel Nevsky established a dynasty in Moscow that eventually became the sovereign power of Russia. Daniel's son, Ivan I, took over in 1328 CE and was permitted by the Mongols to annex territory to Moscow.

This nineteenth-century CE painting depicts the legendary—but probably apocryphal—moment in Russian history when czar Ivan III tore up Russia's letter pledging tribute the Mongols.

Moscow was just one of several almost equally important Russian principalities until the rule of Vasily II, who came to the throne as a ten-year-old in 1425 CE. Vasily used alliances with Lithuania and within the Golden Horde to secure the supremacy of his city.

Moscow's rulers used the fall of Constantinople to the Ottoman Turks in 1453 CE to strengthen their position further. Moscow became regarded by the Russian church and princes as "the third Rome," the true heir to the Byzantine Empire. In 1473 CE, Ivan III, who was grand prince of Moscow from 1462 to 1505 CE, married a niece of the last Byzantine emperor. From 1474 CE, Ivan called himself *czar* (Slavic for "caesar" or "emperor"). He annexed Novgorod in 1478 CE and Tver in 1485 CE. Also in 1485 CE, the Russian princes stopped paying tribute to the Mongols.

This sixteenth-century CE manuscript shows Alexander Nevsky fighting the Teutonic Knights on the frozen Lake Peipus.

Conflicts with the West

Ivan III's successes against the Golden Horde were in stark contrast to the failure of his policies toward the Swedes and the Polish-Lithuanian state. The Russian borders with those realms had no natural frontiers, and any state or organization that had an army and wanted to extend its territory could do so almost with impunity. For example, during the later period of the Kievan state, Russian princes from Novgorod raided what is now Estonia on many occasions. From the early thirteenth century CE, the Teutonic Knights of Livonia (formed in 1237 CE from a previous crusading order, the Brothers of the Sword) became a major power on the Baltic coast. Alexander Nevsky defeated them at the Battle of

Lake Peipus in 1242 CE, but the knights remained a threat until the Lithuanians defeated them at the Battle of Tannenberg (also known as the Battle of Grunwald) in 1410 CE. Lithuania then confronted Russia. Ivan III encouraged attacks against Poland-Lithuania by former subjects of the Golden Horde (such as the Crimean Tartars), but his long wars in the late fifteenth century CE were inconclusive. Similarly, Ivan fought a series of wars against the Swedes who ruled in Finland, but again, there was no decisive success.

Ivan III was succeeded by Vasily III (ruled 1505–1533 CE), who completed the absorption of the old Russian principalities by Moscow, taking control of Pskov in 1510 CE and Ryazan in 1521 CE. There was now a Russian state, with Moscow as its capital, which had a clear unity of culture and language. The birth of modern Russia is conventionally dated to the start of the reign of **Ivan IV** (ruled 1533–1584 CE), also known as Ivan the Terrible. Ivan incorporated non-Slav states into his empire and developed a strong, centralized administrative system for his domain. For these reasons, he is called the first "Czar of All the Russias."

This fourteenth-century CE Persian manuscript depicts Genghis Khan, who united the Mongols and began their period of vast conquest.

CHAPTER SIX

The Mongol Empire

The Mongols, an Asian tribe of nomadic herders, were a force to be reckoned with between the thirteenth and fifteenth centuries CE. Originally based in the grasslands surrounding eastern Asia's Gobi Desert, they went on to build the world's largest land empire. At the height of their power, the Mongols controlled vast expanses of territory, stretching all the way from the Pacific Ocean to the Black Sea. They ruled most of China, and they might have gone on to Europe and the Middle East had it not been for their custom of halting their military campaigns every time one of their khans (emperors) died.

From Temujin to Genghis Khan

The roots of Mongol expansionism can be traced to around 1162 CE, when Yesukai, a Mongol chieftain living near Lake Baikal, fathered a child named Temujin. Yesukai led a loose alliance of around thirty thousand families who sometimes went to war against rival nomads but whose principal activities were sheep farming and hunting.

At age thirteen, Temujin inherited his father's role as tribal chief, but his succession was not unopposed; he was forced into hiding, and on several occasions, he was almost killed by rivals. However, Temujin gave an early demonstration of his skill as a politician and his ferocity as a warrior by overcoming all his adversaries. By 1190 CE, his leadership was acknowledged throughout the greater part of Mongolia.

In 1206 CE, Temujin convened a *kurultai* (gathering of tribal leaders), which he reputedly addressed with these words: "Those who share my fortune, and whose loyalty is as clear as glass, may call themselves Mongols and their power shall be above everything that lives."

Temujin went on to declare the assembly of families, clans, and tribes to be a single nation, and he offered them dominion over the whole world. The gathering then proclaimed him ruler of all the Mongols and conferred on him the title Genghis Khan. "Genghis" is derived from the Chinese word for "valued warrior"; "Khan" comes from the Turkish word for "lord."

From his capital in Karakorum, Genghis Khan announced a simple manifesto—there could be only one ruler, and all opponents would be put to death. He decreed that his successors as khan must be elected, in perpetuity, by the kurultai. That stipulation ultimately had fatal consequences for the Mongols.

Genghis Khan also demanded that no Mongol leader could make peace with an opponent unless that opponent had first acknowledged the authority of the khan. The khan himself acknowledged only the authority of the Great Yasa, a code created by Genghis Khan himself.

The Great Yasa was based on the laws of a Turkic people, the Uighurs, and included some rules that were new to the Mongols but that were of great use to them during the conquests on which they were about to embark. For example, the code permitted Mongols to drink the blood and eat the entrails of animals, practices that had traditionally been forbidden. During the great Mongol expeditions, the blood of horses became an important source of food for the cavalrymen.

Also codified in the Great Yasa was the division of labor between husband and wife. The husband was to hunt and fight, while the wife was to take care of business and the family property.

Every Mongol had equal rights under the Great Yasa. No Mongol was to enslave or fight another Mongol. Horse stealing and adultery, which were regarded as the most serious crimes, were punishable by death. The usual penalty for lesser crimes was flogging. Mongols were not required to pay taxes.

Genghis Khan was a brilliant military commander and strategist. His army was renowned for its organization and discipline. His archers (who used composite bows made of horn and wood glued together) became famous for their accuracy and rapid shooting. At the lowest level, the army was divided into units of ten men, who were obliged to stay together under all circumstances. There was one commander for every hundred men (ten units). Above the commanders were senior officers in charge of every thousand soldiers. The largest unit, known as a *touman*, comprised ten thousand soldiers and was commanded by an *orkon*, a deputy of the khan.

The Mongols originally came from the grasslands surrounding the Gobi Desert.

The Mongols were superb horsemen, and each soldier took at least two or three horses with him on every campaign. The khan's greatest concern was to have sufficient horses for his military requirements. He would often delay attacks for years while he waited to assemble the right number.

During campaigns, the Mongols lived off the land and ate whatever they could scavenge. Most of their horses were mares, and the mares' milk provided a large part of their diet, but on long marches through barren steppes, the men would drink the blood of their horses. Three things about the Mongols particularly amazed their enemies: their endurance, their mobility, and their extreme cruelty to the vanquished.

It is said that Genghis Khan once asked one of his captains what he considered the greatest pleasure for a man. The captain replied, "Hunting with his people in the steppes on a beautiful day with his horse at the gallop."

"No," said the khan. "The greatest pleasure for a warrior is to trample his foe under foot, to seize his horse and riches, and to hear the wailing of inconsolable women." The great khan and his successors certainly embodied that attitude. **Hulagu Khan**, grandson of Genghis Khan, boasted in a letter to Louis IX of France that he was personally responsible for two hundred thousand deaths in his raids into lands that are now part of Iran, Iraq, and Syria.

Genghis Khan's first campaign was against northern China, where the Western Xia people had established their own state. The Western Xia assumed that Genghis Khan would continue to pay tribute to them as his father had always done. When a new Xia emperor, Wai Wang, was crowned, his ministers sent a delegation to Genghis Khan to demand a renewed oath of fealty. The khan treated the Chinese emissaries with scorn. "Let your emperor know that it is a matter of indifference to us whether he regards us as a friend or a foe," Genghis Khan told them. "If he wants to be our friend, then we will let him rule his territory under our authority, but if he would rather have war, then we will fight until one of us is totally destroyed."

After the delegation had departed, the Mongols prepared for war. They collected enormous numbers of horses and made millions of arrows. Around 1200 CE, a well-equipped cavalry army crossed the Great Wall of China. The following years were disastrous for northern China. By 1208 CE, the Mongols were well established in China, although they had difficulty taking some Chinese cities because the cities were fortified with towers and walls. The invaders withdrew to the Mongolian steppes every winter and returned the following summer to continue the invasion.

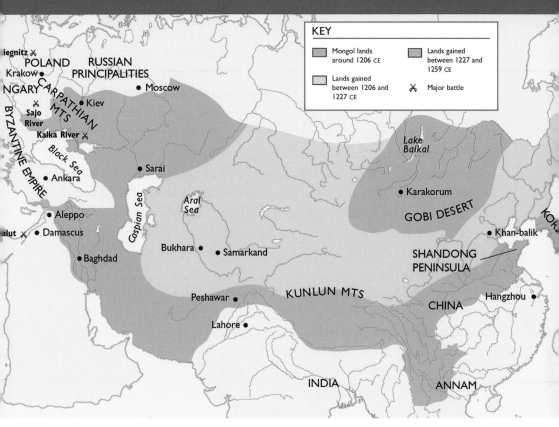

One of Genghis Khan's greatest attributes was his ability to recognize expertise or knowledge that the Mongols did not have. In the same way that he had previously adapted a Turkic legal code, he now hired Chinese generals to teach the Mongols about the technology and tactics of siege warfare. He also employed Chinese bureaucrats who could read and write (most Mongols were illiterate) and knew how to organize the government of a settled society, particularly the collection of taxes.

In 1213 CE, Genghis Khan led his army into the Shandong Peninsula. Within a year, he had conquered the Manchus, who were themselves of Mongolian descent. He took Yenking (modern Beijing) in 1215 CE, razing most of the city to the ground and installing one of his orkons as the city's administrator.

In 1217 CE, Genghis Khan turned his attention to the west. His new target was the powerful Khoresm Empire, based in central Asia and Persia. When the khan was told that the Khoresm Muslims would be more powerful than the Chinese, he assembled his hordes and issued the following warning: "It is necessary for a leader of ten men to be as alert and obedient as the leader of ten thousand men. Anyone who fails in this shall die, together with his wife and children."

The campaigns against the Khoresm emperor Mohammed Shah were remarkable for the speed of Mongol advance and for the khan's bold strategic moves. Cities that surrendered at once, such as Bukhara, were spared, but cities that resisted, such as Samarkand, were sacked and the populations were massacred. During this period, Mongol forces turned south into the Indian Subcontinent to take Peshawar and Lahore. By 1221 CE, the Mongols held sway throughout central Asia and much of Persia.

Another Mongol army then moved through the Caucasus to the mouth of the Dnieper River and crushed a Russian force at the Battle of the Kalka River (near Donetsk, a city in modern Ukraine) in 1223 CE before returning to central Asia.

In 1224 CE, Genghis Khan launched a new campaign in China to break up an anti-Mongol alliance between the Xia and Jin empires. By the time Genghis Khan died in August of 1227 CE, the Mongol Empire covered much of Asia, from the steppes of what is now southern Russia to the China Sea.

Genghis Khan was succeeded by his son Ogotai, who continued the extension of Mongol power, particularly in China. Ogotai was followed by Kuguk and then by Mangu. Mangu was succeeded by his brother **Kublai Khan** (ruled 1260–1294 CE).

The Reign of Kublai Khan

Kublai Khan, a grandson of Genghis Khan, took the Mongol Empire to the height of its power, controlling much of the Eurasian land mass. Before his election as great khan in 1260 CE, Kublai Khan spent seven years with Mangu attempting to complete their grandfather's conquest of China. They fought the Song dynasty in the south and stamped out all resistance in the north.

Although, in theory, Kublai Khan was overlord of the whole Mongol Empire, his principal khanate was China. He established his capital at Khan-balik (modern Cambaluc, near Beijing), where

Marco Polo in China

Marco Polo was born in Venice around 1254 CE. He was the son of Niccolò Polo, a prosperous merchant whose wealth was based on trade with Asia. At the age of seventeen, Marco Polo accompanied his father and his uncle, Maffeo, on a journey to the court of Kublai Khan in China. Once they finally arrived there, they remained for seventeen years. During that time, Marco Polo was often employed by the emperor to travel around China on fact-finding missions, and his written accounts of these journeys have provided much information about the reign of Kublai Khan.

Around 1295 CE, the Polos finally returned to Venice, where they had long been presumed dead. Soon afterward, Marco Polo was captured by the Genoese in a sea battle and put in prison in Genoa. It was there that he dictated his book, *Il Milione* (*The Million*), which was an account (probably much embellished) of his travels through distant lands. Marco Polo was later freed from jail and returned to Venice, where he died in 1324 CE.

There are around 140 manuscript versions of *Il Milione*, and no two have identical text. It is often difficult to sort fact from fantasy, and it is almost impossible to tell which parts Marco Polo himself believed and which were merely reports of popular legends. The most skeptical historians have even doubted whether he went to China at all. Why, for example, does *Il Milione* make no reference to the Great Wall?

One story in *Il Milione* concerns Prester John, the mythical ruler of a Christian kingdom somewhere in the East. According to Marco Polo's account, Genghis Khan asked to marry Prester John's daughter, but the emissaries were arrogantly dismissed with these words: "How does Genghis Khan presume to ask for my daughter's hand when he knows he is only a servant of mine! Leave instantly and never return."

This illustration from a fifteenth-century CE edition of *Il Milione* shows Marco Polo kneeling before Kublai Khan. The golden tablet he is receiving is to be his passport as he travels the realm of the Mongols.

his court became internationally famous. The Venetian merchant-adventurer Marco Polo visited the court, and his memoirs provide insights into the Mongol Empire of the period.

To administer China, the new khan employed a host of talented Chinese and Muslim officials. He adopted the Chinese bureaucratic system but excluded Chinese people from positions of power. The previous Mongol way of life—with its unquestioning obedience to military leaders, reliance on a nomadic lifestyle, and scorn for farmers—did not fit easily into the sophisticated, urban civilization of China. As the caravan routes across central Asia became safe under Mongol control, many more traders and missionaries started to use them. The travelers encouraged increased intercultural contact and understanding but weakened the specifically Mongol way of life.

Kublai Khan's crowning achievement was the unification of China, which he completed in 1279 CE through the subjugation of the Song

Kublai Khan's Palace

While he was in China, Marco Polo lived at the court of Kublai Khan, and his book, *Il Milione*, gives a vivid description of the emperor's palace.

According to one passage: "It is larger than any I have ever seen. The roof—which is adorned with bronze and copper—is very lofty, and the sides of the great halls and apartments are ornamented with gold and silver. There are beautiful representations of warriors, women, birds, and beasts."

He goes on: "The grand hall is extremely long and permits dinners to be served to six thousand people. The palace contains a large number of chambers. The exterior of the roof is adorned with a variety of colors and is painted so well that it shines like gold. The palace grounds are ornamented with many handsome trees and meadows in which are kept various kinds of beasts, such as stags, roebuck, and ermine. In the middle, there is a large lake containing all kinds of fish."

dynasty. Then, Kublai Khan established the Yuan dynasty and became its first emperor.

Kublai Khan then made determined assaults on southeast Asia and forced the kings of Burma, Cambodia, and Annam (the northern part of modern Vietnam) to swear allegiance to him and give him tributes. He sent fleets to Java and Japan but failed to conquer them. Although the Mongol Empire reached its greatest extent under Kublai Khan, the protracted wars were a severe drain on China's (and therefore the Mongols') resources.

Kublai Khan was a Buddhist and made Buddhism the state religion in China, but adherents of other religions remained free to practice them. The emperor encouraged literature and the arts. During his reign, many extravagant buildings were constructed, and the Grand Canal was repaired and extended. Nevertheless, Mongol rule was always resented in China. Chinese officials objected to their reduced status, and the peasants struggled under heavy taxation. Kublai Khan died in 1294 CE, and by the 1340s CE, a combination of crop failures, famine, inflation, and catastrophic floods had led to widespread civil unrest. By the 1360s CE, a former Buddhist monk named Zhu Yuanzhang had gained control of the Yangtze River Valley. In 1371 CE, the Mongols fled back to the steppes.

This sixteenth-century CE manuscript shows the Golden Horde of Batu Khan sacking the Russian city of Suzdal.

Batu Khan Pushes West

The territory that Genghis Khan had wanted to bequeath to his eldest son, Jochi, included all the lands west of the Aral Sea—the open steppes extending from Asia into Europe. However, Jochi predeceased his father, and Jochi's khanate became the realm of his own son, Batu Khan. Because of the magnificence of Batu Khan's camp, this part of the empire became known as the Golden Horde.

Batu Khan was determined to extend his territory. In 1237 CE, he crossed the Ural River to pillage the cities of the Vladimir-Suzdal region in central Russia. In 1240 CE, his armies sacked Kiev and slaughtered its inhabitants. They then went on to Poland and Silesia, where they razed Lublin and Krakow. In 1241 CE, two Mongol columns advanced even farther westward. One column defeated an army of European knights at Liegnitz, west of the Oder River, on April 9. The other column crushed the forces of Bela IV, the Arpad king of Hungary, at the Sajo River on April 11. The Mongols then took the cities of Pest (part of modern Budapest) and

Ragusa (modern Dubrovnik, Croatia). The Mongols were preparing an invasion of central Europe when news reached them in December of 1241 CE that Ogotai had died. Still abiding by the laws of Genghis Khan, they immediately withdrew to Mongolia to help settle the succession.

Although thwarted in its assault on central Europe, the Golden Horde established by Batu Khan extended the khanate from the Ural Mountains to the Carpathians, and from the Black Sea in the south to Siberia in the northeast. The Golden Horde flourished until the end of the fifteenth century CE, when it broke up into the separate khanates of Crimea, Sibir, Kazan, and Astrakhan. Not until 1485 CE did the Russian princes cease paying tribute to the Mongol capital of Sarai on the Volga River.

In the Middle East

The **Il-Khanate**, based in Persia (modern Iran), was established in 1256 CE by Hulagu, who was given instructions, after Mangu's accession, to extend Mongol power into Islamic regions. Hulagu led his horde through Persia, Mesopotamia, Armenia, and Georgia. In 1258 CE, Hulagu and his army stormed the **Abbasid** capital of Baghdad. They razed it to the ground and, according to some accounts, killed more than eight hundred thousand people.

Hulagu then took Aleppo and Damascus. In 1260 CE, however, he was recalled to Karakorum because of the death of Mangu. Once again, the death of a great khan brought an end to a Mongol offensive.

The Mamluk rulers of Egypt took advantage of Hulagu's absence and, at the Battle of Ain Jalut in 1260 CE, defeated the small Mongol army that had been left behind in Syria. On his arrival at Karakorum, Hulagu discovered that his brother, Kublai Khan, had been campaigning successfully in China. The kurultai chose Kublai Khan to replace Mangu. Rebuffed, Hulagu returned to Persia, barely acknowledging the authority of his brother.

In a major example of the forces dragging the greater Mongol Empire apart, there was a short period of hostilities between the Il-Khanate and the Golden Horde. When Ghazan Khan came to power in 1295 CE, he refused outright to acknowledge the great khan. Ghazan

Khan converted to Islam, and the traditional culture of Persia gradually became dominant at court. The power of the Il-Khanate weakened over the years, and when Khan Abu Said died without an heir in 1395 CE, native Persian rule was restored in a number of the small successor states that sprang up.

Tamerlane

In central Asia, Turkic tribes had been dominant until the Mongol conquest. Genghis Khan originally allotted this part of his realm—which roughly corresponds to modern Turkestan—to Jagatai, his second son.

The Gur-e Amir in Samarkand, Uzbekistan, was built as a mausoleum for Tamerlane upon his death in 1405 CE.

After the death of Kublai Khan in 1294 CE, the Turkic peoples began asserting their independence from Mongol authority. The most important Turkic leader was **Tamerlane** (who was also of Mongol descent). Born in 1336 CE, he was nicknamed Timur the Lame because of a crippled leg. He became chief minister to the khan of the Jagatai Mongol realm and then took supreme power for himself around 1369 CE.

Tamerlane, a Muslim, made his capital at Samarkand and then set about enlarging his empire by force of arms. His ambition was to recreate the Mongol Empire as it had been under Genghis Khan. By 1394 CE, Tamerlane had conquered western Persia, Mesopotamia, Armenia, and Georgia. He first allied himself with, and then fought against, the Golden Horde, which never recovered from his ruthless attacks. Tamerlane invaded India in 1398 CE, seizing Delhi and massacring its inhabitants. Moving westward, he attacked Syria in 1400 CE and slaughtered the inhabitants of Baghdad in 1401 CE. Tamerlane then invaded Anatolia (modern Turkey), defeating the Ottoman Turks and taking their capital, Ankara, in 1402 CE.

Tamerlane died in 1405 CE. In 1526 CE, one of his descendants, Babur, founded the Mughal dynasty in India.

The Qarawiyyin Mosque and University in Fes, Morocco, was reconstructed in the twelfth century CE during the reign of the Almoravid dynasty. The school, founded in 859 CE, is often cited as the world's oldest university.

CHAPTER SEVEN

The Islamic World of the Middle Ages

B eginning in the mid-ninth century CE, the strength of the Abbasid caliphate waned, and power in the Islamic world became divided between a number of different groups and regional authorities. For example, the years after 1000 CE saw the rise of the Seljuk and Mamluk empires around the Mediterranean. In spite of the lack of a single centralized power, and in the face of damaging attacks by such peoples as the Mongols, Islam continued to spread as a religion. Indeed, by 1500 CE, the Islamic world was far larger than it had been in previous centuries.

Factors in the Spread of Islam

There were certain important threads running through the Islamic world during the Middle Ages. One was the importance of trade (over both land and sea) in creating rich, prosperous cities that could recover from violent attacks. Islam's reach extended across the Indian Ocean to what is now Indonesia and was well established in the islands of Java and Sumatra by 1500 CE. Islamic traders were also spreading their religion and asserting political control along the coast of eastern Africa.

A second thread was the importance of missionaries in spreading Islam. The most influential missionaries were the Sufis (see sidebar, page 91), members of an Islamic sect that sought direct contact with God. One way of getting into close contact with God was through dance, a practice that has come down to the modern day in the performances of the whirling dervishes. Although Sufis were often distrusted by political leaders within the Islamic world, their piety and asceticism were influential in encouraging conversion to Islam.

Another important thread was the practice of creating armed forces from groups of children who were removed from their families and brought up in closed military societies. Effectively, they were slaves, owing allegiance only to their political masters. Such societies could be extremely effective militarily: the Egyptian-based Mamluks defeated the previously all-conquering Mongols, for example, while the **Janissaries** who served the Ottoman rulers were also very successful. However, these societies could also turn on their masters, as the Mamluks did in Egypt.

Perhaps the most important factor in the continuing expansion of the Islamic world was the attraction that the religion had for many of the groups of people who might otherwise have been its enemies. An example were the Turkic tribes of central Asia. Their fierce and strong nomadic culture made them a threat to the settled societies around them, but most of them had converted to Islam by 1000 CE. One of the first great states to be established by Turkic tribes was the Ghaznavid Empire. Its founder, Mahmud (ruled 998–1030 CE), took over large parts of Afghanistan, eastern Persia, and northwestern India. In Persia, the Ghaznavids were in turn defeated by another wave of Turkic invaders, the Ghuzz Turks. The Ghaznavids abandoned their Persian lands but flourished in northern India. The Ghaznavids were militantly Muslim and destroyed Hindu temples. They were the first of the great Muslim dynasties of India, and they were succeeded by further Muslim states, such as the Ghurid dynasty, the Delhi Sultanate, and finally the Mughal Empire, established by Babur in 1526 CE.

The Seljuk Empire

One Ghuzz Turk clan was particularly successful after moving into the Ghaznavid territories of Persia: the Seljuks. After forcing the Ghaznavids to relinquish control of Persia, the Seljuks took Baghdad. In 1055 CE, they drove out the **Shi'ite** Buyids, who had asserted effective control of the caliphate. Two energetic Seljuk rulers then created a vast empire. Alp Arslan (ruled 1063–1072 CE) conquered

Sufi Muslims

Sufis were Muslim mystics who played an important role in the spread of Islam. The term Sufi probably derives from the Arabic word for "wool," a reference to the harsh woolen robes worn by certain early Muslim thinkers. Sufis were also known as "poor men"—*fakir* in Arabic and *dervish* in Persian. Both of these words have come into use in English.

The ecstatic dancing of Sufi whirling dervishes is a way for them to get closer to God.

Sufism grew out of a desire for a direct connection with God. Meditation on the Koran was an early way of making this connection, but Sufism quickly became associated with mystical poetry.

In Sufi orders and brotherhoods, disciples swore allegiance to "masters" and often lived in the equivalent of monasteries. They undertook missionary activity in central Asia, Africa, and India.

With their commitment to poverty and their strict discipline, Sufis were always an admired religious group, but their importance in the spread of Islam lay in how they expressed feelings during rituals and formal rites of passage, such as marriages or funerals. Dancing, singing, and playing music created an atmosphere that was far removed from the often dry procedures of the more academic Islamic religious figures; the activities made Islam a more approachable religion.

However, the emotional and mystical aspects of Sufism also laid it open to criticism from more conventional Islamic thinkers. Sufis were always at pains to emphasize that they were in complete accord with shari'ah law and were not trying to undercut or ignore it. That said, their mysticism often suggested a feeling that all of creation was one, and this almost pantheistic acceptance of everything in the natural world being of equal value outraged Islamic jurists who based their moral values on a strict interpretation of the Koran.

Syria and then inflicted a heavy defeat on the Christian forces of the Byzantine Empire at Manzikert in 1071 CE. Anatolia, the heart of the Byzantine Empire, now lay open to the Seljuks. Although Alp Arslan was killed fighting against the Qarakhanids (another Turkic people) in 1072 CE, his successor, Malik Shah (ruled 1072–1092 CE) occupied Anatolia and took over Palestine. On Malik Shah's death, the Seljuk Empire stretched from the Aegean Sea through most of what is now Iraq and Iran and on to lands east of the Aral Sea. It had failed to subdue the other major Islamic state in the Middle East (the Fatimids of Egypt) but was otherwise unchallenged.

The Kharaghan towers in northern Iran, built in the eleventh century CE, house the tombs of two Seljuk princes.

This Seljuk state was difficult to maintain as a single entity, however. The range of cultures that it contained— from the sophisticated urban centers of Isfahan and Baghdad to the nomadic tribes of central Asia—had little in common, and the Seljuks were very reliant on Turkic tribesmen who were fiercely independent and mistrustful of any central authority. On Malik Shah's death, two states in Anatolia—the sultanate of Rum (a corruption of the word Rome) and the Danishmend emirate—immediately threw off central authority, and the Seljuk Empire swiftly broke up. This breakup was of great advantage to the invading First Crusaders and enabled the Byzantine Empire to recover some lands in Anatolia.

The Turkic states around Palestine were in disarray until the mid-twelfth century CE, when, under a succession of talented leaders, they retook Jerusalem and asserted their authority over Egypt. The most notable of these leaders was Saladin, who may have been a Kurd. Saladin created his own dynasty, the Ayyubids, who were dominant in Syria and Egypt but were unable to hold on to Persia. Here, a further Turkic state was created—the shahdom of Khoresm.

Northern Africa

While Turkic invaders were proving dominant within the Middle East and northern India, new non-Arab dynasties were also helping to revive Islam in northern Africa. The **Berber** people of northern Africa had taken some time to convert to Islam after the initial Arab conquests, but the **Almoravids** (a Berber dynasty) took power in Morocco in 1071 CE. The Almoravids (the name probably refers to the tightly knit groups into which the Berber warriors were organized) were fierce desert fighters. These ancestors of the modern Tuareg people of the Sahara took Islam south across the desert. The Almoravids then took over the Umayyad caliphate in Spain in 1086 CE and regained swathes of territory that Christian forces had taken after the civil war that had taken place within the Spanish caliphate early in the eleventh century CE. The strength of the Almoravids lay partly in their fierce adherence to Islam, which gave them unity and a cause, but also in their military prowess. They had devised a way of fighting that their enemies had rarely encountered before. Lines of javelin throwers hurled their weapons at the foe and then pulled back to form a solid block of pikemen, who fought rather like the Macedonian phalanx or the Scottish, Flemish, and Swiss pikemen of late medieval Europe. The flanks of this block of pikemen were covered by other light troops and by cavalry mounted on camels. Horses found the camels frightening, so conventional cavalry were unable to break through on the sides of the pikemen. The camels themselves were vulnerable when they charged, but their primary purpose was defensive, and they excelled in this aspect of combat.

In the twelfth century CE, the Almoravids were replaced as standard bearers of Islam in northern Africa and Spain by a second Berber dynasty, the **Almohads**. Originating in a call for renewal of the faith through a purer lifestyle, the Almohads extended their power from Morocco along the shores of northern Africa to as far as Tripoli in what is now Libya. They also became the leading power in Muslim Spain, supplanting the Almoravids in the 1140s CE. However, the Almohads suffered a decisive defeat by Christian armies at the battle of Las Navas de Tolosa in 1212 CE. After that defeat, Christian forces took over large areas of southern Spain, restricting Muslim rule to the southeast, around Granada.

The Mongols Arrive

In the thirteenth century CE, the various states that had developed out of the ashes of the Seljuk Empire faced an enormous new threat. The Mongol forces of Genghis Khan moved out of the great plains of northeastern Asia and became the dominant political and military force over a vast area. Genghis Khan's first major campaign in the Middle East was against the Khoresm state, which he effectively destroyed by 1221 CE. The Mongols then arrived again in force in the early 1230s CE to assert their rule over Persia and Mesopotamia. Seljuk forces from Anatolia were defeated in 1243 CE at Kosedagh, and the Seljuk states there were forced to pay tribute to the Mongols. In 1256 CE, Hulagu (one of the grandsons of Genghis Khan) established the Il-Khanate, based in Persia, and then launched further invasions to the west. However, although Hulagu sacked Baghdad (finally extinguishing the Abbasid caliphate), the Mongols were unable to extend their rule over Egypt or much of Syria, mainly because of the resistance displayed by the rulers of Egypt, the Mamluks.

The Mamluk Dynasty

The Mamluk dynasty ruled Egypt between 1250 CE and 1517 CE. More generally, however, the term Mamluk is used to describe a member of any number of slave armies that existed in the Islamic world in the Middle Ages. Children were received as tribute, bought as slaves, or captured, and then they were brought up as soldiers who owed complete allegiance to their ruler. This practice had been common within Muslim states since as early as the ninth century CE.

The Mamluk children were brought up to obey a strict code called *furusiyya*, which involved obedience to their commanders, loyalty to their comrades, and generosity to women and children. They underwent constant training in the use of weapons and were expert horsemen.

The Ayyubid dynasty in Egypt, established by Saladin in the twelfth century CE, became increasingly reliant on Mamluk support. During the Seventh Crusade, when Louis IX invaded Egypt, the ruling Ayyubid sultan died and a Mamluk took over. He was soon assassinated and eventually replaced by Kutuz, another Mamluk commander. Kutuz founded the Bahri dynasty, named after the

Mamluk "River Island" regiment, which consisted mainly of Kipchak Turks and Circassians.

Fighting with the Mongols

In 1260 CE, the Mongol forces of Hulagu seemed invincible. They had conquered Persia, forced the Turks of Anatolia to pay them tribute, and, in 1258 CE, sacked Baghdad. However, in 1260 CE, the great khan Mangu died, and Hulagu returned to the Mongol capital of Karakorum to help elect Mangu's successor. Hulagu left a subordinate, Kitboga, in control in Syria. Kutuz attacked with a larger Egyptian force and defeated Kitboga at Ain Jalut, thanks to an ambush by Mamluks under the command of Baybars. Baybars then murdered Kutuz and took over control of Egypt. He ruled from 1260 CE to 1277 CE. Baybars was able to withstand further Mongol pressure, partly because he allied with the Mongols of the Golden Horde and through them learned about Mongol fighting methods. He undertook a successful series of campaigns against the crusader states in Palestine. After his death, the campaigns culminated in the fall of Acre in 1291 CE. The crusader states never recovered from this blow.

The Mamluk state was notoriously unstable at the top. There were fifty-five sultans between 1250 and 1517 CE, and fewer than ten of these ruled for more than twelve years. However, the expertise of the Mamluk soldiers in mounted warfare (especially their skill with the composite bow, which the Mongols also used) made them a formidable force. They continued to resist Mongol

This fourteenth-century CE Persian manuscript depicts the fall of Baghdad to the Mongols in 1258 CE.

pressure after Ain Jalut, fighting off a second Mongol invasion at the Battle of Homs in 1281 CE. The Mamluks then defeated Ghazan Khan (of the Il-Khanate) near Damascus in 1303 CE.

Almost a century later, in 1400 CE, the Mamluks were defeated by Tamerlane at the Battle of Aleppo, but fortunately for Egypt, Tamerlane moved north after this victory. Apart from extending their influence north, into Palestine, the Mamluks also attacked south. The Christian state of Maqurrah (in what is now the Sudan) was worn down by Mamluk expeditions; by 1320 CE, it had effectively become a Muslim state.

Mongol Conversions

The spread of Islam as a religion was amply demonstrated as the fourteenth century CE began with the Islamization of much of the Mongol world. By 1300 CE, the rulers of the Il-Khanate in Persia had become Muslim, and the khan of the Golden Horde converted in 1313 CE. The western parts of the Jagatai Khanate of central Asia were also strongly Muslim by the time Tamerlane came to power around 1369 CE.

Ghazan Khan, seen here studying the Koran, converted to Islam in 1295 CE.

The conversion of the Il-Khanate was particularly important. Ghazan Khan's father had gained control of northeast Persia in 1284 CE. Brought up a Buddhist, Ghazan Khan became notable for his interest in the culture of Persia and for his knowledge of many topics that Islamic scholars had researched over the centuries, such as natural history, medicine, and astronomy. He learned various languages, including Arabic, Hindi, and Persian. His conversion to Islam came in 1295 CE, when he was campaigning against Baydu, one of his father's successors. Ghazan Khan's troops are said to

Religious Tensions

In the Middle Ages, the established Islamic world generally had a tradition of tolerance toward other religions, certainly in comparison with the Christian states of western Europe. However, outside this settled world, relationships among different religious groups were less harmonious. In Islamic Spain, for example, the Almohad dynasty, determined to impose a purer and less worldly view of Islam on the Spanish Muslims, proved intolerant of other faiths. The great flowering of Jewish culture within Islamic Spain that had begun around 1000 CE came to an abrupt end in 1148 CE, when the Almohads destroyed the Jewish communities of Andalusia, forcing the Jews to flee.

have converted with him, and the fact that he now led an Islamic army is said to have contributed greatly to his success against Baydu, who was deserted by many of his Persian troops. When in power, Ghazan Khan ruled as a Persian monarch rather than as a Mongol. He specifically encouraged measures that made it more difficult for the newly arrived Mongol aristocracy to arbitrarily exact tribute from settled Persian farmers and towns. In these measures, Ghazan Khan was reflecting an important current that underlay the history of the Islamic world during this period—the conflict between the steppe nomads, who were successful militarily, and the settled agriculturalists and town dwellers, who provided the wealth that the nomads craved.

In some instances, this conflict took an obvious form: nomad armies, such as those of Genghis Khan, Hulagu, or Tamerlane, laid waste to entire cities. The population of Baghdad, for example was massacred twice. In 1258 CE Hulagu's troops devastated the city, and in 1401 CE, Tamerlane's forces did the same. Persia suffered greatly, and some historians claim the population dropped from more than two million to fewer than five hundred thousand as a result of the Mongol attacks.

However, the fate of Persia indicates how complex the relationship between the old civilizations and the violent new arrivals actually was. The Mongols and the Turkic-speaking nomads could not control the societies that they had conquered, so they became dependent upon Persian methods and individuals to rule their new empires. "The Persians ruled for a thousand years and did not need us even for a day. We have been ruling them for one or two centuries and cannot do without them for an hour," one Mongol ruler lamented. Similarly, in Egypt, the Mamluks were a nonnative military aristocracy that depended upon the agricultural riches of the Nile River and the trading expertise of Egyptian merchants for extravagant wealth and abundant military equipment.

The Ghazi Warriors

The conflict between, on the one hand, a sedentary culture in which peaceful relationships predominated and, on the other, a nomadic culture in which violence was accepted (and glorified) as an integral part of life was especially clear in Anatolia. After the Seljuk Turks had defeated the Byzantines at the Battle of Manzikert in 1071 CE, they had been slow to occupy the areas left defenseless. However, the Seljuk sultan was put under great pressure to move into Anatolia by so-called ghazi warriors—groups of Muslim Turkic fighters, often intensely religious in nature, that formed an important part of the Seljuk armies. Fierce, warlike, and brave, these men believed in raiding the infidel and living off the plunder they acquired. Ghazi warriors had first appeared in northern Persia, but they prospered on the borders of the Byzantine Empire during the early period of the Seljuk Empire, conducting raids on the settled farming communities of Byzantine Anatolia.

After Manzikert, the ghazis formed relatively formal brotherhoods that were impossible for Seljukes to control. They attracted misfits of all kinds, and because of their belief in plunder as an integral part of their livelihood, they destabilized whatever lands they lived in. If there was no frontier with the infidel for them to attack, then they tended to attack other Muslim communities. The difficulty for any authorities was that the ghazis had developed a cast-iron rationale for their activities. They represented themselves as the vanguard of the jihad (holy war), in that they were weakening the infidel by their raids, and although Islam forbade the killing of noncombatants, the ghazis believed that enslavement of captives was justified.

The Black and White Sheep

Persia, which had suffered at the hands of Turkic and Mongol invaders in the thirteenth century CE and through the actions of Tamerlane in the fourteenth century CE, was invaded once again by Turkic tribes in the fifteenth century CE. After Tamerlane's death in 1405 CE, various groups vied to inherit his mantle as ruler of central Asia. One group, the Black Sheep Turkomans, were initially based in present-day Azerbaijan. By the middle of the century, they had taken over much of Persia. However, they were attacked by another Turkic group, the White Sheep confederacy. A three-cornered struggle followed, also involving the Safavids, another Turkic tribe based southwest of the Caspian Sea. The White Sheep Turks proved victorious, only to be brought down when they took on the rising power of the Ottoman Empire. Defeated at the Battle of Erzinjan in 1473 CE, the White Sheep Turks were eventually replaced by the Safavids. Shah Ismael I (ruled 1501–1524 CE) created a Safavid dynasty that firmly resisted any further incursions by central Asian tribes and established a secure Persian state.

Anatolia in Disarray

As the Seljuk Empire broke up, the sultanate of Rum and the Danishmend emirate became dominated by ghazi brotherhoods, more so as the Mongol invasions of the thirteenth century CE drove ghazi fighters from Persia and central Asia to take refuge in Anatolia. By the fourteenth century CE, much of Muslim Anatolia was in a lawless state, with small gangs of religiously motivated fighters struggling among themselves and sometimes using the failing Byzantine Empire as an ally in these struggles.

Out of this context, one Turkic leader, **Osman I**, began to build a new empire for himself. Osman came to power in 1281 CE. His domain was a small emirate in western Turkey, but this territory was eventually expanded into one of the world's greatest powers. The new empire eventually took its name, Ottoman, from its first ruler.

This sixteenth-century CE Turkish manuscript shows Sultan Murad I of the Ottoman Empire hunting a wolf.

CHAPTER EIGHT

The Ottoman Empire

The Ottoman Empire developed out of a group of Muslim Turkic tribes in Anatolia during the fourteenth and fifteenth centuries CE. Named for founder Osman I (1258–1324 CE), whose Arabic name was Uthman, the empire grew to be an important world power and lasted all the way until 1922 CE. At its peak, the Ottoman Empire consisted of Turkey, most of southeastern Europe, Israel, Syria, Iraq, parts of the Arabian Peninsula, and much of the northern coast of Africa. The Ottomans were famous not only as fearsome soldiers, but also as great artists and scientists.

The Dawn of an Empire

Osman's father, Ertugrul (died 1280 CE), was chief of a Turkish principality based at Sogut in northwestern Anatolia. Ertugrul was descended from the Kayi, a branch of Oguz Turkmen who had fled the Turkestan region of central Asia to escape the Mongols in the early thirteenth century CE. According to one legend, Ertugrul dreamed that a crescent moon arose and extended from one end of the world to the other. Later, the Ottoman people, interpreting the story as a prophecy of their future greatness, adopted the crescent moon as their symbol.

Ertugrul was given control of Sogut by a Seljuk sultan. It was just one of many small states in the region to be set up by so-called ghazi warriors, who dedicated themselves to fighting the infidel but also fought frequently among themselves. On acceding to power in

Sogut, Osman captured the towns of Eskisehir, Bilecik, Yarhisar, and Yenisehir from the Byzantine Empire. He besieged the Byzantine cities of Bursa and Nicaea (modern Iznik), eventually capturing Bursa just before his death in 1324 CE. A key element in Ottoman success throughout the next 250 years was that Ottoman rulers proved very adept at taking advantage of the weaknesses of their enemies. Osman's initial expansion of his emirate took place in the context of the weakness of the Seljuks, who had been heavily defeated by the Mongols in 1243 CE and were unable to impose unified authority on Anatolia.

Osman's son Orhan (ruled 1324–1360 CE) built on his father's success. Taking advantage of the weakness of the Byzantine Empire, which had never recovered from the sacking of Constantinople by crusaders in 1204 CE, Orhan established a state in the eastern part of what had been Byzantine territory and oversaw Ottoman expansion into the Balkans. He took the city of Nicaea in 1331 CE and Nicomedia (present-day Izmit) three years later. Orhan had a strong sense of religious duty, and he developed Bursa as an Islamic center, building mosques and theological colleges. In 1345 CE, he annexed the rival Turkmen principality of Karasi in western Anatolia. In 1346 CE, Ottoman troops backed the future Byzantine emperor John VI in his struggle against a rival, John V. As a reward, Orhan received the hand in marriage of Theodora (daughter of John VI) and was given leave to conduct raids in Byzantine regions of Thrace and Macedonia. In 1354 CE, Orhan seized Gallipoli, establishing the Ottomans' first permanent holding in Europe.

Toward the end of Orhan's reign, the Ottomans acquired a navy through a daring raid carried out by Orhan's son Süleyman. One night in 1356 CE, Süleyman secretly crossed the Bosporus with an elite corps of sixty soldiers. The troops landed at Tzympe, where they sailed silently away with the Byzantine fleet. By the time the Christians had learned of their arrival, Süleyman and his men had already left. At a stroke, the Ottomans became a major naval power.

Sultan Murad I

Although Süleyman took Tzympe and several other small territories, he never inherited the throne because he died before his father.

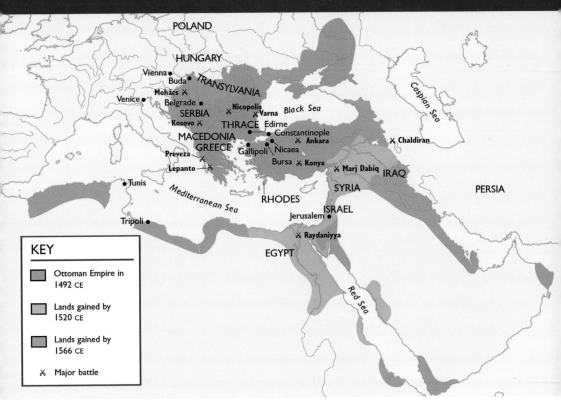

Instead, Orhan was succeeded in 1360 CE by another son, Murad I, the first member of the Ottoman dynasty to use the title sultan. Taking advantage of a fragile Serbian state, which had been in turmoil since the death of Stefan Dusan in 1355 CE, Murad oversaw further Ottoman expansion in the Balkans and Anatolia. In 1361 CE, he took Adrianople and Philippopolis in western Thrace and made the Byzantine emperor John V (who had regained sole power in 1354 CE) into a vassal. Murad established Adrianople as his capital and renamed it Edirne. He also established control of parts of Serbia and Bulgaria, forcing local princes to pay tribute to him. In Anatolia, he defeated a coalition of Turkmen princes at Konya in 13   86 CE.

Murad developed a pragmatic method of dealing with the Christian states in the Balkans. Essentially, he left local rulers in power, provided that they paid tribute and accepted Ottoman control. Christians were not required to convert to Islam, and local customs were left alone. Murad also established a number of Ottoman institutions, such as the Janissary military corps (see sidebar, page 113) and the positions of *grand vizier* (principal minister), *beylerbeyi* (commander in chief), and *kaziasker* (military judge).

Murad died fighting Bulgarian, Serbian, and Bosnian princes at the Battle of Kosovo in 1389 CE; his son Bayezid I succeeded him as ruler.

The Empire Expands

Bayezid I (ruled 1389–1402 CE) put the Ottoman Empire on a firm footing with victories in Europe and Anatolia. He was nicknamed Yildirim (Thunderbolt) for the speed of his conquests. In Europe, he occupied Tirnova (now in Bulgaria) in 1393 CE, conquered Salonika (modern Thessaloniki in Greece) in 1394 CE, and invaded Hungary in 1395 CE—the same year that he began a siege of Constantinople. In response to the threat that the Ottomans now posed to Europe, a number of western states, including Venice and Hungary, launched a crusade. However, Bayezid defeated the alliance decisively at the Battle of Nicopolis in 1396 CE (see sidebar, page 109).

In Anatolia, Bayezid further expanded Ottoman territories, subduing most of the Turkmen principalities. However, this move provoked the anger of the Mongol warlord Tamerlane (also known as Timur the Lame), to whom these rulers in principle owed allegiance. Tamerlane invaded Anatolia and defeated Bayezid at the Battle of Ankara in July of 1402 CE, taking the Ottoman sultan captive. Traditional accounts report that Tamerlane humiliated Bayezid by displaying him in an iron cage and by using him as a footstool. Other stories concern Bayezid's death in captivity the following year. According to some accounts, Bayezid committed suicide by beating his head against the bars of his cage. However, modern historians view these stories as inventions and believe that Bayezid was treated honorably by Tamerlane.

Tamerlane did not attempt to conquer the Ottoman Empire; instead, its administration was left to Bayezid's four sons. The outcome was ten years of civil war. The youngest son, Mehmed I (ruled 1413–1421 CE), finally brought the empire under his control by killing his brothers and fighting off both Christians and Turks in Europe and Anatolia. He died in 1421 CE and was succeeded by his eighteen-year-old son Murad II.

Murad II reestablished Ottoman authority in the Turkmen principalities lost to Tamerlane, and he forced the Byzantine Empire to pay tribute once again. In 1430 CE, he recaptured Salonika from the Venetians. However, he was defeated by an alliance of Hungarians, Serbians, Germans, and others at Jalowaz in 1444 CE. The defeat was only a temporary setback. Later that year, Murad inflicted a heavy defeat on an army of crusaders commanded by Wladyslaw III of Poland that had mounted a siege of the Black Sea port of Varna. This victory brought an end to western attempts to force the Ottomans out of eastern Europe and opened the way to the fall of Constantinople in 1453 CE.

In 1444 CE, before the Battle of Varna, Murad had abdicated in order to lead a life of religious devotion, and his twelve-year-old son **Mehmed II** had temporarily taken control. Nevertheless, Murad, although no longer sultan, led the army that won this famous victory. Murad returned to the throne in 1446 CE and two years later defeated Hungarian commander János Hunyadi at the Second Battle of Kosovo. Following Murad's death in 1451 CE, Mehmed resumed his rule and set about capturing the Byzantine capital, Constantinople.

The Conquest of Constantinople

The city of Constantinople had long been an Ottoman target; it had been besieged five times in the previous sixty-five years. To ensure that the city finally fell into their hands, Mehmed assembled a crack army (estimated at up to 150,000 men), built a huge fleet, and ordered an enormous cannon to be cast. The siege of the city began in April of 1453 CE. At that time, the beleaguered capital of the Byzantine Empire was ruled by the young Constantine XI, whose claim to the throne was contested. Constantine also had little money and few troops. He sought help from the Christian west, but the pope was only willing to call a crusade if the Orthodox Church would merge with the Roman Church. Of all the western powers, Genoa alone responded, sending two ships to Constantine's assistance.

Although they were greatly outnumbered, the city's defenders held out valiantly for several weeks. Neither a heavy artillery bombardment nor an attempt to tunnel under the city's defenses proved successful in breaching the city's boundaries. Eventually, however, the weight of Ottoman numbers caused the Byzantine resistance to collapse.

At dawn on May 29, 1453 CE, Mehmed II, armed with an iron club, led ten thousand Janissaries in a final assault on the city. Behind them came a squad of executioners, who beheaded anyone who tried to flee. Looting began at once. Toward midday, Mehmed made a formal entry into the city, riding on horseback through the Gate of Saint Roman and symbolically proceeding into the Hagia Sophia (the Church of Holy Wisdom, built in the sixth century CE by Byzantine emperor Justinian I).

It was a momentous day. The city established as a "New Rome" and as an eastern center of the Christian faith had fallen to Muslims; henceforth, the city of Constantine would be known as Istanbul and serve as the capital of a Muslim rather than a Christian empire. Mehmed later converted the Hagia Sophia and other Christian churches into mosques.

The Achievements of Mehmed II

Mehmed II conquered Greece, Serbia, Bosnia, Albania, and most of the land around the Black Sea. In May of 1480 CE, he sent a fleet of 170 galleys to besiege the island of Rhodes. For once, he did not get his way; the warrior monks of the Knights Hospitallers, a brotherhood founded in Jerusalem in 1080 CE, had turned the island into an impregnable fortress. The Ottoman fleet besieged the island for more than three months and made three unsuccessful attempts to take it. The Ottomans abandoned the siege in August, having lost nine thousand men in the engagement.

Mehmed's military successes won him the nickname Conqueror, but he was also a well-educated man and an able administrator who rebuilt Constantinople and promulgated the Kanun Nameh, a codification of Ottoman law. He oversaw the compilation of a tax register, in which beys (district administrators) recorded the values and sources of their income, tax rates, and penalties. He also established a group of advisers called the ulama (Arabic for "wise"). These men had all mastered three languages: Turkish, Arabic, and Persian. They were also expert interpreters of the Islamic holy book—

In this nineteenth-century CE French painting, Mehmed II and the Ottoman army triumphantly enter the newly conquered city of Constantinople.

the Koran, from which all matters of law and science were derived in the Ottoman Empire.

The empire that Mehmed created was notable for its religious tolerance, and the major religious groups in the empire had their own form of self-government. This policy paid great dividends. For example, when Mehmed invaded Bosnia, the local Bogomil Christians helped the Ottoman forces against the Catholic army of Hungary.

Bayezid II

Mehmed was succeeded by his son Bayezid II in 1481 CE. Bayezid had outmaneuvered his brother Cem to gain the throne, and Cem had fled. Cem fell into the hands of the Knights Hospitallers and remained in captivity for the rest of his life. Over the course of the next three decades, Bayezid further consolidated the empire, winning great successes against Hungary, Poland, Venice, and the Safavid rulers of Persia.

Bayezid was a learned and pious Muslim, and he poured funds into the building of bridges, hospitals, mosques, and theological colleges within the empire. He promoted law, learning, and poetry, and he took a deep interest in cosmology and philosophy.

In 1511 CE, Bayezid faced a revolt by his sons, Selim and Ahmed, who were also fierce rivals of one other. In April of 1512 CE, having lost the support of the Janissaries, Bayezid was forced to abdicate. He was succeeded by Selim.

Defeating the Mamluks

Selim I (ruled 1512–1520 CE), who was also known as Yavuz (the Grim), established the Ottomans as the leading power in the Muslim world. He first secured the succession, doing away with all possible claimants to the throne, save his son **Süleyman I**. He then attacked Ismael I, the founder of the Safavid dynasty in Persia (modern Iran), which posed a threat to Ottoman stability. Selim saw the Safavid regime as heretical; the Ottomans were followers of mainstream Sunni Islam, while Ismael espoused the Shi'ite form of the religion. At the same time, the Turkmen Kizilbash people, who proclaimed loyalty to Ismael, rose in revolt in Anatolia. Selim crushed the Kizilbash rebellion and then unleashed his cannons to annihilate Ismael at the Battle of Chaldiran, which took place

A Triumph for Bayezid I

In the late fourteenth century CE, the successes of Bayezid I and his Ottoman army in the Balkans caused considerable consternation in the west. As a result, the Byzantine emperor Manuel II and King Sigismund of Hungary persuaded the pope to call a crusade. A huge crusader army containing knights from Burgundy, England, France, Germany, and the Netherlands arrived at Buda in Hungary in July of 1396 CE. Their aim was to drive the Turks out of the Balkans and then proceed across Anatolia and Syria to Jerusalem.

The crusaders advanced across Ottoman-held Bulgaria, massacring thousands of locals—Muslims and Christians—along the way. The crusaders then besieged Nicopolis, the principal Ottoman garrison on the Danube River. Bayezid abandoned his own siege of Constantinople and marched to drive the Christian force from Nicopolis. The speed of Bayezid's response took the crusaders by surprise.

On September 25, the crusaders attacked Bayezid's men. The main section of the Ottoman army was based largely on the top of a hill. Ignoring the advice of their ally Mircea the Elder (the ruler of Wallachia), the heavily armored French and English knights charged up the hill but were forced to dismount by a line of defensive stakes. Upon reaching the top, the exhausted crusaders were slaughtered by the Ottomans, who went on to win the battle.

A small contingent under Sigismund escaped, but the great majority of the surviving crusaders were captured and put to death by Bayezid. The sultan's victory consolidated the Ottomans' already strong position in the Balkans, while keeping up pressure on the beleaguered Byzantine Empire.

Ottoman Governance

By the time of Süleyman I's reign (1520–1566 CE), Ottoman government was organized into four branches or institutions: imperial, military, scribal, and religious. The imperial institution had two sub-branches: an inner service to deal with palace matters and an outer service that had a regulatory function. The military institution, led by the Janissaries and the cavalry, was responsible for defense of the empire and conquest of new territories.

Administration of the empire was the province of the scribal institution. Süleyman established twenty-one virtually independent provinces, which were in turn divided into 250 *sanchaks* (financial administrative districts). The sanchaks were run by an administrative civil service with the authority to collect taxes.

The payment of tax was required of all Muslims. Intended to help the poor, especially with health care and education, tax revenues also paid the ransoms of Ottomans taken prisoner in war, the costs of waging war, and inducements to encourage people of other faiths to convert to Islam.

The religious institution was responsible for Islamic guidance, education, and the administration of justice. Islam is the Arabic word for "surrender," and Islamic religious law and ethics (sharia) assume a willingness to surrender to the will of Allah and to meet social obligations. However, Süleyman did not insist that his subjects convert to Islam; Christians and Jews were free to practice their own religions as long as they paid a special tax (jizyah).

by the Euphrates River on August 23, 1514 CE. Selim then brought the Kurdish and Turkmen principalities in Anatolia into the Ottoman Empire.

In 1516 CE, Selim launched an attack on the Mamluk Empire of Syria, Palestine, Egypt, and Arabia. The word Mamluk means "slave" in Arabic, and the Mamluks were originally enslaved Kipchak Turks (and others) from the area of the Black and Caspian seas. Those slaves were in the service of the Egyptian ruler, but in 1250 CE, they had rebelled and created their own government and empire. Although individually the Mamluks were fearsome warriors, the Ottoman armies were well organized tactically and their use of cannons was extremely effective. Selim defeated the Mamluks in two great battles—at Marj Dabiq (near Aleppo in Syria) on August 24, 1516 CE, and at Raydaniyya (near Cairo) on January 22, 1517 CE. Syria, Egypt, and Palestine were then subject to Ottoman rule.

Süleyman in Hungary

Süleyman I succeeded his father, Selim, in 1520 CE and reigned until 1566 CE. In the course of his forty-six-year rule, he brought the Ottoman Empire to its peak, crossing the Danube River to take Hungary, seizing the area of Anatolia that remained outside Ottoman influence, and capturing parts of Iraq. His realm ran from the Balkans to the Middle East and Persia; in Arabia, it included the coasts of the Red Sea and the Persian Gulf.

John Sigismund, seen here kneeling before Süleyman I, ruled parts of Hungary as a vassal state of the Ottoman Empire.

On land, Süleyman fought repeatedly in Hungary. He first invaded in 1521 CE, seizing the city of Belgrade (then a possession of the Hungarians). When Süleyman returned in 1526 CE, he killed the Hungarian king, Louis II, and defeated the Hungarian army at the Battle of Mohács. In 1529 CE, he supported John Zápolya, the lord of Transylvania who had been elected king by Hungarian nobles, against a challenger, Austria's Hapsburg archduke Ferdinand I. Süleyman drove Ferdinand back into Vienna and then unsuccessfully besieged the city. Following John Zápolya's death in 1540 CE, the Austrians invaded Hungary again, provoking Süleyman to take action once more. He captured Buda (across the Danube from the city of Pest, and now part of the

Süleyman I and his architect, Mimar Sinan, were responsible for a flourishing of construction projects during the sixteenth century CE, including the eponymous Süleyman Mosque in Istanbul.

Hungarian capital Budapest) and incorporated the middle Danube region into the Ottoman Empire, leaving the Hapsburgs in control in northern Hungary and allowing Transylvania limited freedom as a vassal state under the rule of John Zápolya's son John Sigismund.

Süleyman also fought three campaigns against the Safavid dynasty of Persia between 1534 CE and 1555 CE, during the course of which he captured Iraq. He signed a peace treaty with the Safavids in 1555 CE.

Fighting on the Mediterranean

At sea, Süleyman's fleet came to dominate the Mediterranean region. In 1522 CE, he drove the Knights Hospitallers from the island of Rhodes, forty-two years after they had defied the invasion attempt of Mehmed II. Süleyman unleashed four hundred ships carrying an army of two hundred thousand men against a defending force of seven thousand. Despite this inequality of numbers, the siege lasted six

The Janissaries

The elite Ottoman military unit of the Janissaries was established by Murad I in the fourteenth century CE. The unit's name is a Latin corruption of the Turkish *yeni cheri*, meaning "new army." Murad used unconventional methods of recruitment for his army; he demanded Christian children from Balkan provinces as tribute, put them in training camps, and indoctrinated them in Islam. This method of recruitment, called *devshirme* (from the Turkish for "gathering"), was common throughout the fifteenth and sixteenth centuries CE. The Janissaries, eventually numbering forty thousand, played a large part in the success of the Ottoman Empire. They did, however, represent a risk; in the seventeenth and eighteenth centuries CE, a Janissary revolt was always enough to bring down a sultan.

The Janissary corps was abolished in 1826 CE. Janissaries attempted to revolt in that year, and the sultan, Mahmud II, unleashed a cannonade on their barracks. Most members of the elite corps were killed, and the remainder were disbanded.

months, but the Ottomans finally prevailed. Süleyman was generous in victory, allowing the surviving defenders to leave Rhodes for Malta, which was part of the kingdom of Sicily at that point.

A series of strategically important naval victories followed. At the Battle of Preveza, fought off the Greek coast in 1538 CE, an Ottoman fleet defeated a combined force from Spain, Genoa, Venice, the Papal States, and Malta. The victory gave the Ottomans control of the eastern Mediterranean region. Süleyman's domain eventually reached to northern Africa, where he captured Tripoli in 1551 CE and defeated a Spanish campaign in 1560 CE.

Arts and Administration

Süleyman was called "the Magnificent" abroad, but at home, he was known as "the Just" or "the Lawgiver" because of his development of the legal system of Mehmed II. He appointed very able statesmen and

Barbarossa and the Ottoman Navy

Under the leadership of the great admiral Khayr ad-Din (ca. 1478–1546 CE), the Ottoman navy achieved a position of dominance in the Mediterranean Sea that lasted from the 1530s CE until the navy's defeat at the Battle of Lepanto in 1571 CE. The admiral, originally called Khidr, was given the name Khayr ad-Din (Greatness of the Faith) by Süleyman I. In the west, Khayr ad-Din was known as Barbarossa (Red Beard).

This painting depicts the Battle of Preveza, an important victory for Khayr ad-Din and the Ottoman navy.

Khayr ad-Din was born on the Aegean island of Lesbos. He was the son of a knight who had fought for Mehmed II in the capture of the island from the Genoese in 1462 CE and then stayed there. Khayr ad-Din began life sailing as a privateer, capturing Algiers in 1516 CE. In 1529 CE, Süleyman made Khayr ad-Din the Ottomans' admiral-in-chief, and in 1534 CE, he captured Tunis for the empire. In 1535 CE, Holy Roman emperor Charles V recaptured Tunis. However, in 1538 CE, Khayr ad-Din won a major victory over Charles's fleet at the Battle of Preveza. The victory assured Ottoman dominance in the Mediterranean. In 1540 CE, Charles tried to persuade Khayr ad-Din to abandon the Ottomans and serve the Holy Roman Empire instead, offering him the position of admiral-in-chief and possession of all Spain's territories in northern Africa. Barbarossa refused.

Khayr ad-Din continued to terrorize western-held islands and coastal possessions on the Mediterranean until he retired to Istanbul in 1545 CE. He built a palace on the Bosporus shore but died the following year.

religious advisers—grand viziers (ministers) such as Rustem and ulama such as Kemalpasazade. Another trusted advisor was Roxelana, one of Süleyman's wives.

Süleyman had total authority over imperial resources. He acquired huge estates from the rulers he vanquished in the course of his conquests, and then he leased them to his followers—vassals with essentially no independent political power. Under the Islamic laws of inheritance, women were not permitted to come into possession of land, so when a family of vassals died out, the estates reverted to the sultan.

Süleyman was a great patron of architecture, and he was given the epithet "the Magnificent" because of the sacred and secular buildings he had built in Istanbul and in other cities of the empire. In particular, he oversaw the design and construction of several of the superb creations by the architect Mimar Sinan, including the Sehzade Mosque and the Mosque of Süleyman in Istanbul—both of which are considered to be masterpieces. Süleyman was also a great patron of other arts, including poetry. The sultan financially supported a large number of artistic societies; records reveal that at any one time up to six hundred artists and craftsmen could be employed by the palace.

Süleyman the Magnificent died on September 5, 1566 CE, while on campaign in Hungary. He was succeeded by his son Selim II.

This terra-cotta figure is a relic of the Nok culture, which emerged in central Nigeria around 500 BCE.

CHAPTER NINE

The Cradle of Civilization

Africa is known as the cradle of civilization. The world's first hominids (forerunners of humans) emerged there around four million years ago, primarily in the southern and eastern central parts of the continent. Known as *Australopithecus* (southern ape), these hominids walked on two legs, unlike their apelike ancestors who moved on all fours. They were up to 4.5 feet (1.4 m) tall and had brains that were 35 percent the size of modern human brains. Archaeologists have found australopithecine skeletons in present-day Ethiopia and South Africa, though they may have inhabited other parts of Africa as well.

Around two million years ago, *Homo habilis* (skilled man) and *Homo erectus* (upright man) evolved. Skeletal remains of the two groups dating from 1.7–1.8 million years ago have been found in Tanzania and Kenya. Homo erectus was around 5 feet 10 inches (1.79 m) tall and had brains that were 75 percent the size of modern human brains. *Homo sapiens* (thinking man) emerged around one million years ago and gradually evolved into *Homo sapiens sapiens*, the earliest modern human, who appeared around 100,000 BCE. The oldest identifiably human remains, dating from around 120,000–90,000 BCE, have been unearthed in Ethiopia and Tanzania and on the border between Swaziland and South Africa.

Hunting and Gathering

The earliest *Homo sapiens sapiens* lived by hunting and gathering. They hunted gazelle, eland, and quagga (a species of zebra, now extinct) and foraged for grubs and plants. They traveled great distances in small family groups, camping in caves or beneath small clumps of trees. They used stone tools, and they were making bows and arrows by around 15,000 BCE. (Some inhabitants of the region—notably the Khoikhoi and the San in the Kalahari Desert—have maintained this lifestyle into the twenty-first century CE.)

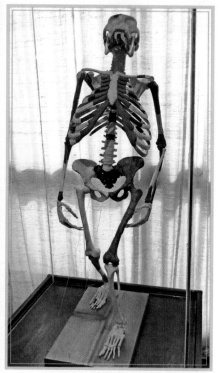

This skeleton is a reconstruction of Lucy, a 3.2-million-year-old *Australopithecus* specimen unearthed in Ethiopia.

In the equatorial rain forests of the Congo River Basin, other groups of hunter-gatherers emerged. Among them were the Twa and the Mbuti, diminutive humans with an average height of 5 feet (1.5 m). Their descendants remain there in the modern era. (Genetically distinct non-African pygmies, probably also of archaic origin, live in Asia and Oceania.)

The Birth of Agriculture

Around 13,000 BCE, climate changes in northern Africa caused desertification and led to a sharp decline in the number and variety of wild animals. The human population of the region responded by developing a new culture based on the gathering of wild grains, which they threshed with stone sickles and crushed with grinding stones. The culture spread through northern Africa and along the eastern coast of the Mediterranean Sea into Palestine, Syria, Mesopotamia, and Persia. In an effort to regularize their supply of food, the indigenous peoples began to raise plants and domesticate goats, sheep, cattle, and donkeys. The same period saw the emergence of the Afro-Asiatic family of

Africa's Geography and Topography

The continent of Africa occupies 11.7 million square miles (30 million square kilometers), one-fifth of Earth's total land area. To the west, it is bounded by the Atlantic Ocean, to the east by the Red Sea and the Indian Ocean, to the north by the Mediterranean Sea, and to the south by the confluence of the Atlantic and Indian Oceans off the Cape of Good Hope. Africa contains a wide variety of terrains, ranging from tropical forest to desert, from snowcapped mountain ranges to vast, flat savannahs.

Africa is divided into three main regions: the Northern Plateau, the Eastern Highlands, and the Central and Southern Plateau. The bulk of the Northern Plateau is occupied by the Sahara, a desert that covers 3.5 million square miles (9 million sq km), more than one-quarter of the continent. To the northwest, the desert gives way to semiarid steppes and the rugged peaks of the Atlas Mountains in Morocco and Tunisia. To the southwest lie the Fouta Djallon highlands, and to the south lie the mountains of Cameroon.

The fertile plateau of the Eastern Highlands runs down the eastern coast of Africa, from the Red Sea to the Zambezi River. The plateau is the highest part of the continent, with an average elevation of more than 5,000 feet (1,500 m). The Great Rift Valley, running 3,000 miles (4,830 km) from Syria to southeastern Africa, cuts through the Eastern Highlands. The Nile River—the world's longest—rises in the Eastern Highlands and flows northward to the Mediterranean through a chain of lakes in the Great Rift Valley.

The Central and Southern Plateau, which covers most of southern and western central Africa, contains the Congo River and the Kalahari Desert. The Congo River Basin consists of more than 1.6 million square miles (4.1 million sq km) of dense equatorial rain forest. The Kalahari Desert covers 275,000 square miles (712,250 sq km). It is mostly arid red soil, although there are expanses of sand in the east. West of the Kalahari, the temperate Namib Desert extends 1,200 miles (1,930 km) along the southwestern coast of Africa. The Namib is cooled by the offshore Benguela Current. In the extreme south, the High Veld is an arid area that covers much of South Africa.

This prehistoric cave painting, depicting a hunting scene, was found in the Tassili region of present-day Algeria.

languages, a group that includes the Coptic (ancient Egyptian) and Semitic tongues.

Later, from around 9000 to 2000 BCE, there was a prolonged period of abundant rainfall in eastern Africa. As a result, the region was distinctly different from the desert that covers much of it today; the landscape was characterized by wooded hills, green valleys, and rolling plains. The topography engendered a water-based culture that spread across northern Africa from the Atlantic Ocean to the Nile River and south to the lake country in eastern Africa. Around 8000 BCE, hunters and gatherers yielded the most fertile areas of Africa to peoples who had developed new techniques of agriculture and animal husbandry. Those peoples, who spoke languages of the Nile-Saharan group, also manufactured pottery. They lived mainly in encampments, which they used for gathering seasonal crops or hunting, but they also had some permanent settlements. In the Tassili region of the central Sahara, these peoples left thousands of wall paintings that depicted their lifestyle. The primitive art provides much valuable information about the people's methods of herding and hunting (particularly gazelles, giraffes, and elephants) and their rituals, which featured music and dancing.

The period of abundant rainfall ended around 2000 BCE, and within two hundred years, the greater part of northern Africa had been

San Rock Art

The San bushmen, who now live in the Kalahari Desert, created a major legacy in painted and carved rock art at around fifty thousand sites across most of the southern half of Africa. The San roamed freely over a vast region for thousands of years before they were largely confined to the Kalahari Desert by **Bantu** settlers around 400 CE. There are major concentrations of San art in the Drakensberg Mountains in South Africa, in the Matobo Hills in Zimbabwe, in the Tsodilo Hills in Botswana, and at Twyfelfontein in Namibia.

Some examples of San art are extremely old. One rock in the shape of a snake and cut with marks that look like scales may date from 75,000 BCE. Slabs of rock painted in charcoal, white, and ocher were found in a cave in the Hun Mountains of southwestern Namibia and were dated to 25,000 BCE. At one time, these paintings, which show both animals and humans, were believed to be scenes of everyday life, but they are now thought to be religious paintings made by shamans (tribal spirit guides or religious leaders). The shamans would have used the images to record visions they had in the spirit world and to bring their people into contact with supernatural forces. The shamans and their followers believed that the images had the power to promote rainfall, bring healing to the sick, or deliver prey to the hunters. Depicted animals include the eland, the hippopotamus, the elephant, and the giraffe. The pictures rarely represented the kinds of animals that the San bushmen habitually ate, such as tortoises and small antelopes.

transformed into a vast desert. As the region's inhabitants adapted to the hotter and drier environment, they concentrated on the crops that produced the greatest food yield for the least physical work. The particular crops varied by region.

Early Social Structures

Studies of present-day hunter-gatherer groups by anthropologists have yielded valuable clues to the social organization of their prehistoric African forebearers. In light of the research, it is likely that the early hunter-gatherers had strong social bonds designed to maintain group identity. Their core values were equality and communal sharing. Decisions were reached by negotiation rather than imposed from above by leaders. The hunting was probably carried out by the men, and the foraging was performed by the women. Because hunting was considered more important than gathering, the men were accorded higher social status.

With the transition to an agrarian lifestyle, new social structures probably evolved in order to manage the larger groups living in permanent or semipermanent settlements. Groups of people were probably identified on the basis of collective identity as descendants of a common ancestor. Genealogy was traced either from a male ancestor (patrilineal descent) or from a female ancestor (matrilineal descent). As lineage began to play a more important role in the organization of food production and society, leaders—and especially the elderly—were accorded higher status than other members of the group. Marriage arrangements became important economic and political factors.

From Stone to Iron

In many parts of the world, human evolution progressed from the Stone Age (during which people made tools from stone), through the Bronze Age (when tools and weapons were made of bronze, an alloy of copper and tin), to the **Iron Age** (when iron was used). In Africa, however, development did not always conform to the same pattern. Although bronze was made and used to a limited degree in northern Africa around 2000 BCE and there was a flourishing copper industry in southern Congo at the start of the first millennium BCE, the continent as a whole did not pass through a Bronze Age; it generally moved straight from stone to iron.

By around 700 BCE, iron was already in use in the lower reaches of the Nile River (the northern part of modern Egypt), to which it had been brought by the Assyrians, and in Carthage (a city in modern Tunisia), to which it had been brought by the Phoenicians. Africa's earliest indigenous iron-making culture was that of the Nok in central Nigeria (ca. 500 BCE–200 CE). Nok artisans were renowned for their life-size terra-cotta sculptures in addition to their iron artifacts (see

Nok Statuary

The Nok culture existed on Nigeria's Benue Plateau from around 500 BCE to around 200 CE. The culture was characterized by superb life-size terra-cotta statues of people and animals. Unfortunately, most of the statues survive only in fragments. The culture takes its name from the village of Nok, where the first terra-cotta pieces were unearthed during tin-mining operations in 1928 CE. Four years later, eleven statues in immaculate condition were discovered near Sokoto in northwestern Nigeria. Other remains were subsequently found over a wide area, and the culture is believed to have extended over a region measuring 200 miles (320 km) north to south and 300 miles (480 km) east to west.

The Nok artisans exhibited extraordinary skill in their modeling. Some of their statues were more than 4 feet (1.2 m) tall. The statues have well-defined characteristics and few stylistic differences. These facts suggest that the modelers may have been working in a well-established artistic tradition whose earlier manifestations are lost. The artisans also made iron tools (among the first in Africa), as well as stone ornaments and stone tools (including axes).

sidebar, page 123). Subsequently, from around 200 CE, the use of iron became widespread among other cultures in eastern and central Africa.

During the first four centuries of the Common Era, the practices developed by the early agrarian and Iron Age societies spread, through human migration, to other parts of Africa. The migrants organized themselves into units of increasing size, and political leaders became more and more important as early African kingdoms developed.

Bantu Expansion

Through the study of African languages (see sidebar, page 125), historians have hypothesized that a vast migration of speakers of Bantu languages took place over the course of hundreds of years, beginning in the first millennium BCE and continuing until around 400 CE. The evidence suggests that the Bantu moved south from their original homeland in the

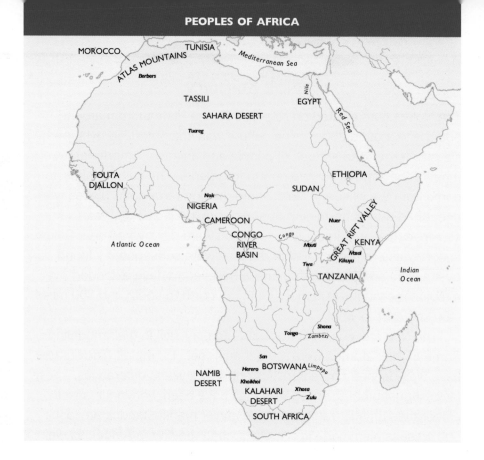

lower Niger region and divided into eastern and western branches. The eastern Bantu migrated through what is now Zimbabwe, crossing the Limpopo River into South Africa. Their descendants include the Kikuyu, Shona, Xhosa, and Zulu peoples. The western Bantu moved down the Atlantic coast and then inland to become the ancestors of the Herero and Tonga peoples.

The Bantu were pastoralists, herders, and cattle breeders. Their advanced techniques of farming and iron making enabled them to dominate the cultures they encountered. They probably learned their iron-making techniques from the people of the Nok culture. It is possible that the spread of Bantu languages was caused not by a vast human migration but rather by a cross-fertilization of culture through a small number of travelers or by intermarriage.

As they or their culture spread, the Bantu displaced the indigenous hunter-gatherer peoples of the Khoikhoi and the San. Both peoples adopted aspects of the Bantu culture but retained their own language, Khoisan.

African Language Groups

Today, there are more than a thousand languages in Africa. Most of them are spoken by no more than two hundred thousand people, although fifty languages are used by more than five hundred thousand people. Writing systems exist for only around half of these languages, which have no early literature but are noted for their ancient oral traditions. Their alphabets were created in the nineteenth century CE by Christian missionaries, who adapted the Roman alphabet to the sounds they encountered. On the basis of the spread and development of languages, historians have traced the development of African cultures and the movement of peoples. The four principal groups of African languages are Afro-Asiatic (Hamito-Semitic), Nilo-Saharan, Niger-Kordofanian, and Khoisan.

The Afro-Asiatic (Hamito-Semitic) family includes the ancient Egyptian language, written in hieroglyphics, and Tamarshak, spoken by the Berbers of the Atlas Mountains and the Tuareg of the Sahara. As the name suggests, Nilo-Saharan languages developed in the upper valley of the Nile River, the Sudan, the Sahara, and eastern Africa. A key subgroup is the Nilotic languages, which are spoken by two large cattle-based cultures—the Nuer and the Masai.

The Niger-Kordofanian group is the largest of the four language families of Africa. The group includes the languages of the Bantu peoples. Niger-Kordofanian languages are divided into two subgroups: the Niger-Congo family and the Kordofanian family. The Niger-Congo languages spread across virtually all of Africa south of the Sahara; the Kordofanian languages, which include Swahili, are used only in southern Sudan. Khoisan, the language of the Khoikhoi and San hunter-gatherer peoples, is the smallest of the African language families. It is sometimes called the click language because it is characterized by distinctive clicking sounds made with the tongue. Khoisan is spoken today by around a hundred thousand people, primarily the Khoikhoi and San of southern Africa. The click has spread through cultural and linguistic contact into a number of Bantu languages, including Xhosa, Zulu, and Sotho in South Africa and Dahalo in Kenya.

In this scene, painted on a wooden casket found in the tomb of King Tutankhamen (ruled 1332–1323 BCE), the Egyptians fight with their neighbors, the Nubians.

CHAPTER TEN

The Tribes, Kingdoms, and Empires of Africa

T he continent of Africa has seen the rise and fall of countless cultures and empires, from ancient kingdoms such as Nubia, Aksum, and Ghana, to comparatively recent powers such as the Ashanti and Zulu peoples. Many of these societies grew wealthy through long-distance trade. They could boast rich cultural traditions and highly skilled craftspeople. For centuries, Africa remained largely self-governed, but the acceleration of European colonialism in the nineteenth century CE radically changed the political situation on the continent.

Nubian Civilization

The first great civilization of tropical Africa was the kingdom of Nubia, which was created around 1000 BCE by the peoples of the middle part of the Nile River Valley (now part of Sudan). The area, a major source of gold, had previously been dominated for 1,800 years by the Egyptians, who called it the Land of Kush. In the eighth century BCE, the Nubian king Shabaka conquered Egypt and established the twenty-fifth dynasty of pharaohs, who held power for around fifty years. However, in 671 BCE, the Assyrians attacked Egypt, seizing control of the empire and driving the Nubians back to the Land of Kush.

From the Assyrians, the Nubians learned how to make iron. The first capital of the Nubian kingdom had been established on a bend of the Nile River at Napata, around 250 miles (400 km) north of Khartoum, an area rich in iron ore. By the sixth century BCE, however, the region was becoming overexploited; there was little wood left for burning to smelt iron ore. Consequently, Napata was replaced as the capital by Meroë, a site farther up the river, only around 125 miles (200 km) north of Khartoum.

The Nubians controlled major trade routes along which they sold iron, gold, ivory, and elephants—not only in Africa but also to Greece and Rome. The kingdom's power increased in direct proportion to its wealth. In 24 BCE, the Nubians destroyed two Egyptian outposts of the Roman Empire, at Philae and Aswan, thereby forcing a border agreement between Nubia and Roman Egypt. (The Greek historian Strabo later wrote that the assault on Philae had been made by a "Queen Candace," but he had mistranslated Candace, a Nubian word for "queen" rather than a personal name; the word merely indicated that a female ruler had led the attack.)

The power and influence of Nubia in the first century CE is evidenced by its exchange of ambassadors with the Roman emperor Nero (ruled 54–68 CE). Its heyday was brief, however. The Nubian Empire soon crumbled, losing much of its territory to desert nomads, notably the Blemmyes of the Arabian Desert. Around 350 CE, Meroë was overrun by Ezana, king of Aksum, a realm on the Ethiopian Plateau.

The people of Nubia were converted to Christianity in the sixth century CE and proceeded to establish the kingdoms of Nobatia, Mukurra, and Alodia. All three realms were conquered by Arabs in the fourteenth century CE, although Alodia resisted until the sixteenth century CE. Egypt regained control of the former Nubian region in 1820 CE.

The Kingdom of Aksum

The ancient kingdom of Aksum, in the northern Ethiopian highlands, was founded around 50 CE by the Amhara, a people of partly Semitic origin. The rulers of Aksum established the Solomonid dynasty, which claimed descent from the biblical king Solomon.

According to legend, the people of Sabaea, a Semitic kingdom of southern Arabia, had migrated across the Red Sea to Ethiopia at the start of the first millennium BCE. Their ruler, Makeda (the biblical queen of Sheba), was said to have known Solomon (a tenth-century BCE king of Israel) and to have borne him a son, who became Menelik I ("Emperor and King of Kings of Ethiopia" and the ancestor of the Solomonid rulers). All Ethiopian emperors claim descent from Menelik in the royal line of the Lion of Judah.

The Aksumite Empire was established by 100 CE. The foundation of its commercial success was ivory, of which it had an abundant supply. From its main port, Adulis (modern Massawa) on the Red Sea, Aksum forged strong trading links with Greece, Rome, and India. Many of the proceeds were spent on the construction of great palaces and temples. From the third century CE to the sixth century CE, Aksum also dominated Yemen on the Arabian Peninsula.

In the fourth century CE, Ezana of Aksum (the king who overran Meroë in Nubia) made Christianity one of the state religions—after he himself had been converted by two Syrian Christians, Frumentius and Aedesius. Surrounded at first by pagans and then by Muslims, the Aksumite Empire fought wars for religious as well as economic reasons. In the seventh century CE, Aksum declined, but its kings retained power through alliances with the Byzantine Empire. In the tenth century CE, the Solomonid dynasty was toppled by the Zagwe, the ruling family of Lasta, a kingdom of the Central Plateau region.

Ghana

In western Africa, a succession of states became rich and powerful through their control of trade routes across the Sahara. Ghana, the region's first great empire, emerged in around 400 CE out of the Iron Age culture of the Nok people. The empire lay between the upper Senegal River and the Niger River, northwest of the modern country of Ghana. Extending from Timbuktu on the Niger to the Atlantic Ocean, ancient Ghana was well positioned for trade. Its lands roughly covered what is now eastern Senegal, western Mali, and southeastern Mauritania.

The empire—known locally at the time as Wagadou (Land of Herds)—later became known as Ghana because that was the word for "king" in the Wagadou language. Ghana prospered most between the eighth and eleventh centuries CE. Its gold, mined in the Wangara region in the Senegal basin, was transported north, where it was traded for Saharan salt. Ghana also exported kola nuts, ivory, and slaves.

At stations along the trade routes, it imposed taxes on salt, textiles, copperware, Egyptian horses, and tools, some of which came all the way from Europe. Ghana also established an extensive system for the collection of income tax.

Ghana reached its peak under the Soninke elite, around 1050 CE. However, the capital city was conquered and plundered in 1076 CE by the Almoravids (a militant Muslim sect of the Sanhaja Berbers in Morocco), and the empire disintegrated as the peoples of western Africa withdrew their allegiance and formed independent kingdoms. Around 1200 CE, people from Takrur, a rival state in western Africa, took control of Ghana. They were then themselves challenged by the Malinke people of Kangaba, another kingdom in the region. In 1235 CE, the Malinke king Sundiata Keita defeated the Takrur at the Battle of Kirina and razed the capital at Kumbi Saleh. Sundiata Keita then founded the kingdom of Mali, which became the main power in the region.

The Kings of Mali

The founding of the kingdom of Mali by Sundiata Keita was immortalized in the oral tradition by griots (itinerant singer-poets) of the Malinke, a subgroup among the Mandé people of western Africa.

Sundiata Keita (Mari Jata; Mari the Great), a Muslim who had come to the throne of a small state on the upper Niger River in 1230 CE, expanded his new empire by conquering the neighboring tribal domains. He made his own birthplace, Niani (near the border of Mali and Guinea), the capital of the empire. He introduced cotton cultivation and textile manufacture, but his empire's main strength lay in trade; his traders established posts throughout western Africa, creating links to the long-distance trade routes between Asia and Africa and, via the Mediterranean, to Europe. Sundiata Keita also developed an efficient system for taxing trade.

In 1255 CE, Sundiata Keita drowned while attempting to get across the Sankarini River. He was succeeded by a line of capable Muslim Mali kings, the greatest of whom was his great-nephew Mansa Musa (ruled 1312–1337 CE), who conquered the cities of Timbuktu and Gao, and expanded the Mali Empire. Mansa Musa was a devout Muslim who went on a widely celebrated hajj (pilgrimage) to Mecca, a journey

An Account of Ghana

The capital of the Ghana Empire was described in *The Book of Roads and Kingdoms*, written around 1068 CE by El Bekri, a geographer from Córdoba, Spain. He wrote: "Ghana consists of two cities situated on a plain. One, inhabited by Muslims, is very large and has twelve mosques. The city where the king resides lies at a distance of 6 miles (10 km) and is called al-Ghaba, which means 'the forest.' The region between the two cities is covered with houses built of wood and stone."

El Bekri's account was based on tales he had heard from traders who had been in the region. The first city mentioned by El Bekri was the base for merchants. The second city, in addition to being the site of the royal palace, was the setting for religious rites. The two cities ultimately merged into one. Most of the houses were made of wood and clay, but some of the wealthier merchants lived in stone dwellings. At its peak, the capital had a population of thirty thousand people. El Bekri described the government and religion: "The king has interpreters, a treasurer, and chooses most of his viziers [advisers] from among the Muslim population. The [non-Muslim] religion is pagan and consists of idol worship."

El Bekri also gave details of the empire's wealth: "All gold nuggets found in the mines belong to the king, but he gives the gold dust to his subjects." Of the empire's military strength, El Bekri states: "The king of Ghana can raise an army of two hundred thousand men, forty thousand of whom are armed with bows and arrows." Other reports indicate that the people of Ghana lived in great luxury, wearing woolen, silk, and velvet clothing. The king's palace had the finest sculpture, painting, and glasswork; his stables contained hundreds of horses, which walked on carpets and were tied with silken ropes.

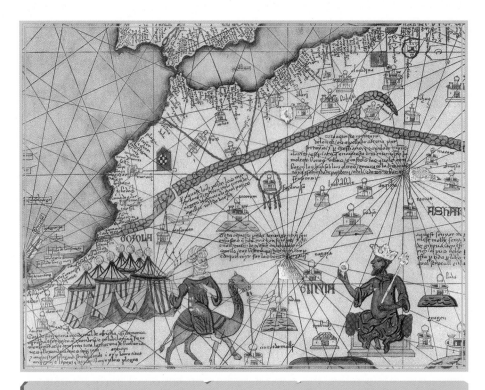

This medieval Catalan map of northwestern Africa includes a portrait of Mansa Musa (*lower right*), king of the Mali Empire.

he undertook at the head of a vast caravan comprising hundreds of camels and thousands of people. In July of 1324 CE, he passed through Cairo, where he distributed so many gifts of gold that he caused inflation throughout Egypt. On reaching Mecca, he met the Arabian poet and architect Es Saheli and persuaded him to travel to Mali. Es Saheli encouraged Mansa Musa to import Muslim teachers and to build schools, including a university in Timbuktu.

An eyewitness account of the Mali Empire in the mid-fourteenth century CE was written by Ibn Battuta of Tangiers, an Arab traveler who had visited India, China, Indonesia, and Turkestan before arriving in Niani in 1353 CE. By that time, Mansa Musa had been succeeded by his son, Mansa Maghan (ruled 1337–1341 CE), who had then been succeeded by Mansa Musa's brother, Mansa Süleyman (ruled 1341–1360 CE). Ibn Battuta reported: "The sultan's daily dress is a red velvet tunic. He is preceded by musicians, who carry gold and silver guitars, and followed by three hundred armed slaves. When he sits down, they play trumpets, drums, and horns." He praised the locals' belief in justice and their strong sense of law and order: "Complete freedom reigns in the land. Neither travelers nor the inhabitants have reason to fear robbers or violent men."

In the mid-fifteenth century CE, the Mali Empire was eclipsed by the **Songhai Empire**, which became the preeminent trading state in western Africa until around 1600 CE. A smaller Mali kingdom continued to exist.

The Songhai Empire

The Songhai people originally made their capital at Gao as early as the seventh century CE. The city grew rich on trade but was conquered and incorporated into the Mali Empire by Mansa Musa in 1325 CE. However, Songhai rule was reestablished there in the fifteenth century CE, and under Sunni Ali (ruled 1465–1492 CE), the kingdom of the Songhai became a great empire. Ali (also known as Ali the Great) incorporated eastern Mali and the central Niger region into his empire. Supported by a powerful army and a navy on the Niger River, he captured the trading city of Djenné in 1473 CE.

Ali was succeeded in 1493 CE by one of his generals, Muhammad Touré, who ruled as Askia Muhammad I until 1528 CE. (The name Askia, meaning "the forceful one," was reputedly given to him by one of Sunni Ali's daughters.) Askia Muhammad extended his empire by conquest eastward as far as Lake Chad and westward almost to the Atlantic Ocean. Around 1500 CE, he captured Agadez (in modern Niger), an important city at the convergence of trade routes to and from Tripoli and the Nile River Valley. He seized the salt mines under the control of Agadez and had irrigation canals constructed to turn parts of the desert into arable land. Agadez was also an important post for the trade in slaves, who were sold to Arabs farther north.

In 1513 CE, Askia Mohammad extended his control of trade routes by annexing Kano (a city on the Hadejia River), which was important for the trade in leather, gold, salt, ivory, and slaves. He introduced bureaucratic government, standardized trade regulations, and oversaw the policing of the trade routes.

Askia Mohammad also promoted literacy and learning across the empire. He was a devout Muslim who, in 1496 CE, had made a hajj to Mecca, where he had been appointed caliph (Islamic leader) of western Sudan. Under him, Timbuktu enjoyed a great flowering of literature and Muslim scholarship and became an even greater cultural center than it had been under the Mali.

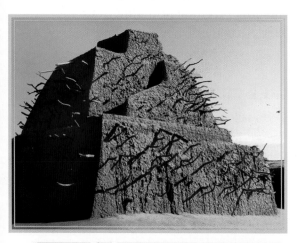

The Tomb of Askia in Mali is thought to be the resting place of Askia Mohammad, king of the Songhai Empire.

In 1528 CE, when he was more than eighty years old, Askia Mohammad was deposed by his son. Askia Mohammad is believed to be buried in a mud-built monument in Gao known as the Tomb of Askia. The monument includes two mosques, a cemetery, and an assembly ground, as well as a pyramidal tomb.

Indigenous authors rose to prominence during the time of the Songhai Empire. Ahmad Baba (1556–1627 CE) wrote works on Islamic law that are still referred to today. Other scholars translated the works of ancient Greek authors, such as Plato and Aristotle, and wrote treatises on astronomy and mathematics. Lost for hundreds of years, the works were rediscovered in 1851 CE in the Baguirmi area, south of Lake Chad.

The Songhai Empire endured until 1591 CE, when it was toppled by a cavalry invasion by Moroccans in search of gold mines. Minor kingdoms such as Gonja, Ségou, and Kaarta arose, vying to fill the power vacuum left by the Songhai. None of those states achieved dominance, however.

Kanem and Bornu

The Kanem Empire was established to the northeast of Lake Chad and built its prosperity on the trans-Saharan trade route that carried ivory and slaves to the region surrounding Tripoli (in modern Libya).

The first Kanem rulers were the Zaghawa (or Duguwa), the dominant members of a confederation of nomads. They were succeeded by the Sayfuwa, who converted to Islam around the time that they took power in the eleventh century CE. The Sayfuwa expanded their lands through conquest, and by the thirteenth century CE, the Kanem Empire extended as far as Kano (in modern Nigeria) to the west, Wadai (in modern Chad) to the east, the Fezzan region (in modern Libya) to the north, and the Adamawa grasslands (in modern Cameroon) to the south. The capital of the Kanem Empire was Njimi.

In the fourteenth century CE, the Bulala people (from the region of Lake Fitri in central Chad) drove the Sayfuwa rulers westward into the Bornu region (to the west of Lake Chad). Initially, the Sayfuwa lived as nomads, but around 1472 CE, their *mai* (ruler), Ali Dunamami, established a new fortified capital at Ngazargamu (in modern Nigeria) and began to build the Bornu Empire.

Under Ali Gaji (ruled 1497–1515 CE), the Sayfuwa recaptured Njimi but continued to rule from Ngazargamu over the Kanem-Bornu Empire. Idris Alooma (ruled 1571–1603 CE) greatly increased imperial power using military camps, scorched-earth tactics, Berber camels, and musketeers armed with weapons purchased from the Ottoman Turks. Idris Alooma took control of the trade routes to Egypt. He was also a notable diplomat who established links with Egypt and Tripoli as well as with the Ottomans. After Idris Alooma's death, the power of the empire faded in the seventeenth century CE, but it survived in a weakened form until 1846 CE, when it was taken over by the Wadai Empire to the east.

Other Kingdoms of Western Africa

The Hausa peoples established several independent city-states that survived from the late ninth century CE to the late sixteenth century CE and peaked around 1400 CE. Lying between the Songhai on the Niger River and Kanem-Bornu in the region of Lake Chad, the Hausa city-states were Biram, Daura, Zaria, Rano, Gobir, Katsina, and Kano; the last two were major urban centers of commerce, made rich by trans-Saharan trade. In the fourteenth century CE, they all converted to Islam and were repeatedly subjected to conquest by the larger kingdoms of western Africa.

The Edo (or Bini) peoples founded the kingdom of Benin in the twelfth century CE. From a capital at Benin City, their obas (kings) ruled over most of what is today southern Nigeria. Oba Ozolua (ruled ca. 1480–1504 CE) established a slave trade with Portugal that continued until the eighteenth century CE. Benin was annexed to British Nigeria in 1897 CE.

These metal staff figurines are artifacts of the Yoruba people of western Africa.

The Ashanti peoples formed a confederation in the early eighteenth century CE. Their kingdom, in what is now central Ghana, reached its peak around 1750 CE. As they tried to subdue the rival Fanti peoples, the Ashanti encountered the British and fought against both until 1826 CE. The Ashanti capital, Kumasi (now in Ghana), was burned in 1873 CE during another round of fighting with the British. Prempeh I, head chief of the Ashanti from 1888 CE, was captured in 1896 CE and exiled by the British to the Seychelles (a group of islands in the Indian Ocean), but he was reinstated in 1926 CE.

The Yoruba peoples established the kingdom of Oyo in territory between the Volta and Niger Rivers around 1400 CE. They created an empire that flourished around 1650 to 1750 CE, but by the early nineteenth century CE, it had collapsed into several small kingdoms and eventually fell under British control.

The kingdom of Dahomey was founded on the coast of the Gulf of Guinea in the early seventeenth century CE. It expanded from its capital, Abomey, in the eighteenth century CE and profited from the slave trade, notably under Agaja (ruled 1708–1732 CE), who seized the coastal town of Allada and traded directly with European slave merchants. Gézo (ruled 1818–1858 CE) added inland territory as the French arrived on the coast. The French later defeated Béhanzin (ruled 1889–1894 CE), and the kingdom became part of French West Africa. In 1960 CE, the colony gained independence as the Republic of Dahomey; in 1975 CE, it was renamed Benin.

East African Peoples

In eastern Africa, Bantu tribes arriving around 1000 CE assimilated the indigenous San peoples. Arab traders established ports, colonized the coast, and intermarried with the Bantu population, developing a new culture and language—Swahili. They established several coastal city-states, including Mogadishu, Mombasa, Malindi, Lamu, Kilwa, Pate, and Sofala. The ruling Arab Africans grew rich exporting gold, ivory, and slaves (many of them Bantu).

Inland, peoples of unknown origin moved down the Nile River to settle in the interlake areas and establish complex societies in the fourteenth century CE. The Bachwezi dynasty created a kingdom between Lake Victoria and Lake Edward in the late fourteenth century CE. Luo people from Sudan took control of the kingdom around 1500 CE. They drove the Bachwezi south to the kingdom of Rwanda, which had been established in the fifteenth century CE by the indigenous Bututsi peoples. The Luo then established the kingdoms of Ankole and Buganda (parts of modern Uganda) and Karagwe (part of modern Tanzania). In Rwanda, the Bachwezi established rule over the Bututsi by the sixteenth century CE.

Kingdoms of Central Africa

Having discovered major deposits of gold and grown rich through trading, the Karanga people (descendants of the Bantu) established the Mwene Mutapa Empire around 800 CE. The Karanga civilization was the earliest and most advanced in the region, and it endured for a thousand years. At its height (ca. 1450–1500 CE), it ruled over the lands between the Zambezi and Limpopo Rivers (modern Zimbabwe and Mozambique).

The Karanga began building Great Zimbabwe, a city and religious center, around 1100 CE. Construction was not completed until the fifteenth century CE, by which time Great Zimbabwe was probably home to around eighteen thousand people. Today, the ruins—17 miles (28 km) southeast of Masvingo—cover 100 acres (40 hectares), and most of them are still contained by a stone wall that is 30 feet (9 m) tall. The word *Zimbabwe*, which gives its name to the modern nation, probably means "stone houses."

The Mwene Mutapa Empire declined sharply in the sixteenth century CE before disintegrating through factional fighting. In 1629 CE, it became a vassal state of Portugal. Thereafter, survivors of the ruling dynasty established a new kingdom called Karanga in Mozambique; it survived until 1902 CE.

In western central Africa, the kingdom of Kongo was established in the fourteenth century CE. At the height of its power, around 1500 CE, it governed land stretching from the Atlantic Ocean to as far east as the Kwango River and from the Congo River in the north to as far south as the Kwana River. The kingdom fell to Portuguese slave traders in the seventeenth century CE.

In the heart of central Africa, to the east of Lake Tanganyika, the Luba people under chief Kongolo embarked on the creation of the Luba Empire around 1500 CE. The empire's economic strength, based on trading copper and palm oil, was at its height under a succession of strong rulers between 1780 and 1874 CE. In the late nineteenth century CE, the Luba Empire was conquered by Belgium. It then became part of the Congo Free State and later part of the Belgian Congo before becoming independent in 1960 CE as the Democratic Republic of Congo.

Around 1600 CE, one of the sons of the Luba chief Kongolo founded a separate dynasty and a new state, the Lunda Empire, on the southern border of his father's domains—on lands that are now part of the modern Democratic Republic of Congo, northeastern Angola, and northwestern Zambia. The Lunda Empire eventually divided into the states of the Bemba, Kasanje, and Kazembe. The largest of these states was Kazembe, which was dominant from 1750 to 1850 CE. In the late nineteenth century CE, the Lunda Empire

The ruins of Great Zimbabwe are a reminder of the Mwene Mutapa Empire of the Karanga people, which reached its peak in the fifteenth century CE.

was divided among three European colonial powers: the Portuguese in Angola, the Belgians in the Congo Free State, and the British in northwestern Rhodesia.

The Zulus and Other Southern Tribes

After around 1000 CE, the indigenous Khoikhoi and San peoples of southern Africa were dominated by Bantu immigrants. The descendants of the eastern branch of Bantu were the Shona, Xhosa, Kikuyu, and Zulu peoples, while the descendants of the western branch were the Herero and Tonga peoples.

This nineteenth-century CE photograph shows Moshesh (*seated, center*), founder and leader of the Basotho kingdom.

The Zulu leader **Shaka** (ca. 1787–1828 CE) created an empire in southern Africa. At the start of his rule, in 1816 CE, Shaka attempted to unite the neighboring Bantu tribes in what is now the South African province of KwaZulu-Natal. When that plan failed, he took up arms against them and unleashed the *mfecane* (Zulu for "crushing"), an era of warfare during which many indigenous peoples were expelled from their lands.

The period of social dislocation and migration that followed led to the creation of several new kingdoms. Tribes left the Zulu area in all directions. Sobhuza, chief of the Ndwandwe peoples, went north and established the Swazi kingdom. Another chief, Moshesh, formed the Basotho kingdom in what is now Lesotho. Another Ndwandwe chief, Soshangane, led his fighting men into what is now Mozambique, where he defeated the Tsonga people and established an empire that he named Gaza, after his grandfather. The Gaza Empire survived until 1895 CE, when it fell to the Portuguese. The Kololo chief Sebetwane traveled north and seized the region of Barotseland (now part of western Zambia). In 1837 CE, the Ndebele chief Mzilikazi Khumalo invaded the southern part of the Mwene Mutapa Empire and established Matabeleland (now part of western and southwestern Zimbabwe).

The Zulus themselves stayed in their own territory, but the increasingly large European presence in the region eventually led to their downfall. They held on, in the face of an onslaught of white intruders eager to exploit the mineral resources of southern Africa, through the reigns of three kings—Dingane (ruled 1828–1840 CE), Mpande (ruled 1840–1872 CE), and Cetshwayo (ruled 1872–1879 CE).

In the end, the Zulus were defeated by the British. European colonial dominance of the region would continue well into the twentieth century CE.

CHRONOLOGY

ca. 4 million BCE
Early hominids emerge in eastern and southern Africa.

ca. 2 million BCE
Homo habilis and *Homo erectus* evolve.

ca. 100,000 BCE
First modern humans develop in Africa.

ca. 15,000 BCE
Bows and arrows first used in Africa.

ca. 2000 BCE
Bronze Age begins in northern Africa.

ca. 1800 BCE
Previously fertile Sahara becomes desert.

ca. 1000 BCE
Nubia gains independence from Egypt. Copper industry flourishes in southern Congo.

ca. 700 BCE
Iron Age begins in Egypt.

ca. 50 CE
Aksum emerges in Ethiopia.

ca. 200 CE
Iron Age methods spread to eastern and central Africa.

ca. 300 CE
Slavs start to settle in Russia.

330 CE
Byzantium renamed Constantinople.

381 CE
Arian heresy condemned at Council of Aquileia.

395 CE
On death of Theodosius I, Roman Empire divided into eastern and western empires.

ca. 400 CE
Ghana develops into an empire.

443 CE
Constantinople threatened by Attila the Hun.

476 CE
Last Roman emperor, Romulus Augustulus, deposed by German invaders.

ca. 550 CE
Kiev emerges as leading city in Russia.

629 CE
Mohammed leads first pilgrimage to Mecca.

793 CE
Vikings raid monastery on Lindisfarne off the English coast.

800 CE
Charlemagne is crowned
Holy Roman emperor.

847 CE
End of iconoclasm.

860 CE
Harald Finehair inherits small
kingdom; eventually becomes first
sole king of Norway.

865 CE
Vikings capture Eboracum
(modern York), England.

867 CE
Basil I founds
Macedonian dynasty.

ca. 878 CE
Danelaw created in
English midlands.

885 CE
Viking forces lay siege to Paris.

911 CE
Danish Viking Rollo becomes
first duke of Normandy.

982 CE
Erik the Red reaches Greenland.

988 CE
Russia adopts
Orthodox Christianity.

ca. 1000 CE
Mahmud begins campaigns in
Persia, Afghanistan, and India

that lead to creation of
Ghaznavid Empire.

1016 CE
England united with
Denmark and Norway
under Cnut the Great.

1018 CE
Bulgaria becomes part of
Byzantine Empire.

1071 CE
Turks defeat Byzantine forces at
Battle of Manzikert.

1095 CE
First Crusade proclaimed by
Pope Urban II.

1099 CE
Crusaders succeed in
taking Jerusalem.

1145 CE
Second Crusade launched by
Eugenius III.

1147 CE
Crusader army defeated by Turks
at Battle of Dorylaeum.

1187 CE
Saladin captures Jerusalem. Pope
Gregory VIII calls Third Crusade.

1198 CE
Pope Innocent III initiates
Fourth Crusade.

1204 CE
Constantinople sacked during Fourth Crusade.

1235 CE
Kingdom of Mali founded in western Africa.

1240 CE
Kiev sacked by Mongol army.

1244 CE
Turkish and Egyptian forces take Jerusalem.

1250 CE
Mamluks take power in Egypt.

1256 CE
Il-Khanate established.

1258 CE
Osman I, founder of Ottoman Empire, born. Mongols sack Baghdad.

1260 CE
Mongols defeated by Mamluks at Battle of Ain Jalut.

1281 CE
Osman I takes control of small emirate in Anatolia, sowing seeds for Ottoman Empire.

1290 CE
Mamluk dynasty ends in Egypt.

1313 CE
Khan of Golden Horde converts to Islam.

1360 CE
Murad I takes power; Ottoman Empire expands into Balkans and Anatolia.

1382 CE
Moscow captured by Mongols of the Golden Horde.

1396 CE
Bayezid I defeats Christian alliance at Battle of Nicopolis.

ca. 1400 CE
Hausa and Yoruba peoples dominate along Niger River.

1402 CE
Tamerlane defeats Ottomans at Battle of Ankara.

1410 CE
Lithuania defeats Teutonic Knights at Battle of Tannenberg.

ca. 1450 CE
Songhai succeeds Mali in western Africa.

1453 CE Constantinople falls to Ottoman Turks.

1485 CE
Russia ends tributes to Mongols.

1521 CE
Ottoman army under Süleyman I takes city of Belgrade.

1520 CE
Süleyman I takes power in Ottoman Empire; arts and culture flourish during his forty-six-year reign.

1522 CE
Ottomans drive Knights Hospitaller from island of Rhodes.

1533 CE
Accession of Ivan the Terrible, first "Czar of All the Russias."

1538 CE
Ottoman fleet commanded by Khayr ad-Din defeats Christian fleet at Battle of Preveza.

1555 CE
Süleyman signs peace treaty with Safavids.

1566 CE
Süleyman I dies.

1591 CE
Songhai conquered by Moroccans.

ca. 1600 CE
Dahomey founded in central Africa.

1750 CE
Ashanti dominate central Ghana.

1879 CE
The British defeat Zulus.

GLOSSARY

Abbasids Dynasty of caliphs formed by descendants of Mohammed's uncle Abbas; ruled from Baghdad (750–1258 CE) until it was sacked by Mongols. Accorded a purely religious function in Egypt, Abbasids held power there from 1261 to 1517 CE.

Albigensians Christian heretics in southern France in the twelfth and thirteenth centuries CE; the target of the Albigensian Crusade in 1209 CE, they were finally destroyed by the Inquisition.

Almohads Islamic reformers from northern Africa who drove the Almoravids out of southern Spain in 1146 CE, establishing a strong caliphate.

Almoravids Fundamental Muslim tribe from the southern Sahara who conquered northern Africa and aided the Muslims in Córdoba against the Christians between 1086 and 1146 CE.

Anatolia Another name for Asia Minor (part of modern Turkey).

Arian heresy Doctrine of fourth-century CE theologian Arius; held that Jesus Christ was not of the same substance as God, but merely the best of created beings.

Australopithecus "Southern ape"; an upright-walking hominid from around four million years ago; found in Africa.

Bantu People of Africa, south of the equator, who speak related languages. After around 1000 BCE, they occupied large portions of Africa, leaving the area around Lake Chad and mixing with agricultural people.

Berbers Descendants of the pre-Arab inhabitants of northern Africa.

Bosporus Strait, 19 miles (30 km) long, that joins the Black Sea and the Sea of Marmara.

Bulgars People of Bulgaria, a region and nation of the Balkans that constituted the strongest empire in eastern Europe in the ninth and tenth centuries CE. Incorporated into the Byzantine Empire in 1018 CE, the Bulgars rebelled in 1185 CE, forming another empire, which collapsed in the fourteenth century CE.

Byzantium Ancient Greek city on the shore of the Bosporus; later known as Constantinople; modern Istanbul.

caliph From *khalifah*, Arabic for "successor"; religious and political leader of Islam; successor to Mohammed. Competing caliphs divided the Islamic states.

caliphate Office and realm held by a caliph.

Cathars Heretical Christian sect that flourished in western Europe in the twelfth and thirteenth centuries CE. The Cathari believed that there are two principles, one good and one evil, and that the material world is evil.

Constantinople Name for Byzantium (present-day Istanbul), which became the (Christian) residence of the emperor Constantine in 330 CE. In 395 CE, it became the capital of the eastern Roman Empire.

Danelaw Viking kingdom in northeastern England.

Eboracum Roman name for their fortification in northern England; later became the Viking town of Yorvick and finally the modern city of York.

Fatimids Shi'ite dynasty of caliphs in northern Africa (909–1171 CE); descended from Mohammed's Fatima; conquered Egypt and founded Cairo around 969 CE.

Fifth Crusade (1217–1221 CE) Expedition that conquered Lisbon in 1217 CE and Damietta in Egypt in 1219 CE. Against the pope's wishes, the crusaders tried to conquer Egyptian territory in exchange for Jerusalem, but their attempt ended in failure.

First Crusade (1095–1099 CE) Led by Godfrey of Bouillon and Raymond of Toulouse; conquered Edessa, Tripoli, Antioch, and Jerusalem, making them Christian kingdoms.

Fourth Crusade (1202–1204 CE) Expedition by French knights; captured Byzantium with the aid of Venice and founded a western-style empire.

Golden Horde Western part of the Mongol Empire. At its peak, it included most of European Russia.

Homo erectus Hominid that walked upright and lived between 500,000 and 150,000 years ago in Africa, Asia, and Europe; used tools, made shelters, and utilized fires.

Homo habilis Hominid that walked upright and lived around two million years ago, at the same time as *Australopithecus*; first hominid species to be found in association with manufactured tools.

Huns Central Asiatic people noted for horsemanship and ferocity in battle; drove the Visigoths from Ukraine (ca. 370 CE); conquered eastern and central Europe in the fifth century CE; seized western Europe under Attila (ca. 450 CE).

iconoclasm Policy of destroying religious images (icons); introduced in the eighth century CE by the Byzantine emperor Leo III.

Il-Khanate Mongol dynasty that ruled in Persia in the thirteenth and fourteenth centuries CE.

Iron Age Period during which major tools and weapons were made of iron; while many cultures arrived at the Iron Age via the Bronze Age, many African civilizations skipped the Bronze Age and moved straight from using stone to using iron.

Islam Monotheistic religion worshipping Allah; founded by Mohammed in the seventh century CE. Its tenets are recorded in the Koran.

Janissaries Army of slaves and Christian prisoners of war who were indoctrinated with Turkish culture and military discipline. They stood as the basis for Turkish military success between 1360 and 1826 CE. Regular outbreaks of Janissary revolts took place from the seventeenth century CE onward. Their power ended in 1826 CE when Sultan Mahmud II had them massacred.

Kiev Capital of the Russian Empire of Vladimir and Yaroslav; flourishing trade center and seat of the Byzantine Church; located in present-day Ukraine.

Knights Hospitaller Society of Christian knights who fought the Muslims. The order grew out of the eleventh-century CE pilgrims' hospital in the Holy Land and gradually took on a military character.

Knights Templar Religious military order established at the time of the crusades to protect Christian pilgrims to the Holy Land. The order was destroyed in 1307 CE.

Mamluks Originally, slaves hired as mercenaries by caliphs in Cairo to maintain order in the twelfth century CE; gained power in 1250 CE; dominated Egypt until the start of the sixteenth century CE.

Mongols Asian tribes of horsemen who originally came from lands to the north of China;

united by Genghis Khan in 1190 CE; conquered central Asian Islamic states, China, Russia, and the Delhi Sultanate in the twelfth and thirteenth centuries CE.

Moscow City that became the seat of Byzantine Russian Christianity after the fall of Kiev. Moscow separated from the Mongols in the fourteenth century CE and assumed the leadership of all the Russian principalities. After the conquest of Byzantium, Moscow became the new Christian center.

Nika Revolt Uprising (January 13–18, 532 CE) in Constantinople of the Greens and the Blues, who turned the population against Justinian. The population appointed a new emperor and destroyed the city center. Belisarius suppressed the revolt with mercenaries.

Novgorod Russian trading post and manufacturing center for the German *hansas*, which monopolized trade in the North Sea and the Baltic Sea. Novgorod came under Mongol threat in the thirteenth century CE. Ivan III conquered the city in 1478 CE.

Pechenegs Seminomadic Turkic people who occupied the steppes to the north of the Black Sea; became a threat to Byzantium in the tenth century CE.

Second Crusade (1145–1148 CE) Authorized by the pope after the Turks had conquered Edessa and threatened Jerusalem. The Christians unsuccessfully besieged Damascus and returned home empty-handed.

Seljuks Turks who named themselves after their deceased leader; captured Baghdad from the Shi'ites; established power in Persia around 1055 CE; conquered Anatolia in 1071 CE. Their kingdom disintegrated by the end of the twelfth century CE.

Shi'ites Supporters of Mohammed's son-in-law Ali; seceded from orthodox Islam after the murder of Hussein in 680 CE. Shi'ites (from shi'ah, Arabic for "partisan") believe that their leaders (imams) are divinely guided and have the right to Muslim leadership.

Songhai Empire State in western Africa (present-day Mali, Niger, and Nigeria) that flourished as a trading nation in the fifteenth and sixteenth centuries CE.

Teutonic Knights Order of knights in northern Germany and the Baltic states. Founded in 1198 CE, they were defeated by Lithuania at the Battle of Tannenberg in 1410 CE. By the end of the fifteenth century CE, they had lost their political influence.

Third Crusade (1187–1192 CE) Followed the capture of Jerusalem in 1187 CE. Frederick I Barbarossa, Philip II Augustus, and Richard the Lionheart traveled to Palestine. Christians conquered the fortress of Acre, but Jerusalem remained in Turkish hands.

MAJOR HISTORICAL FIGURES

Alexius Comnenus Byzantine emperor between 1081 and 1118 CE; partially restored the strength of the empire after losses to the Normans and the Turks in the eleventh century CE.

Alfred the Great King of Wessex, a Saxon kingdom in southwestern England, between 871 and 899 CE; prevented England from falling to the Danes.

Alp Arslan Seljuk sultan who ruled between 1063 and 1072 CE; conquered Georgia, Armenia, and much of Asia Minor.

Attila the Hun King of the Huns between 434 and 453 CE; conquered western Europe; defeated in Gaul by Romans and Visigoths in 451 CE; plundered Italy in 452 CE.

Charlemagne Frankish king from 768 to 814 CE; founded the Holy Roman Empire, which he led from 800 CE.

Cnut (died 1035 CE) Danish king who united Denmark, England, and Norway into a single kingdom; also known as Canute.

Constantine the Great Roman emperor between 306 and 337 CE; ruled initially in the west only but became absolute sovereign in 324 CE; built Constantinople; legalized Christianity.

Eriksson, Leif (ca. 970–1020 CE) Norse explorer; first European to reach the shores of North America.

Genghis Khan (ca. 1162–1227 CE) First leader to unite the Mongols; led campaigns to conquer parts of China and the Islamic world.

Hulagu Khan Grandson of Genghis Khan; founded the Il-Khanate dynasty in 1256 CE; seized and sacked Baghdad.

Ivan IV (the Terrible) First "Czar of All the Russias"; ruled 1533–1584 CE; introduced an effective central administration and created an empire that incorporated non-Slav states.

Kublai Khan Mongolian general and statesman; grandson of Genghis Khan; ruled 1260–1294 CE. He conquered China and became the first emperor of its Yuan, or Mongol, dynasty. In that role, he promoted the integration of Chinese and Mongol civilizations.

Leo III Byzantine emperor between 717 and 741 CE; sometimes known as Leo the Isaurian; gained the throne after several succession conflicts; made the Byzantine Empire a buffer against Islamic expansion.

Mehmed II Sultan of the Ottoman Empire; nicknamed the Conqueror, he was responsible for many successful military campaigns, including the taking of Constantinople in 1453 CE. He also oversaw important administrative reforms.

Osman I Founder of the Ottoman Empire; ruled 1281–1324 CE.

Richard I the Lionheart King of England; ruled 1189–1199 CE; took part in the Third Crusade.

Shaka (ca. 1787–1828 CE) Founder and leader of the Zulu Empire in southern Africa. When he failed to unite all of the region's tribes, he oversaw the *mfecane*

(crushing), during which many indigenous peoples were expelled from their lands.

Süleyman I Sultan of the Ottoman Empire; ruled 1520–1566 CE; conquered Rhodes and Belgrade; reorganized the state and tolerated different religions.

Tamerlane (Timur the Lame) Mongolian ruler between around 1369 and 1405 CE; subjected the Mongols in the west; conquered territory in Persia, India, and Syria; spread Islam.

Tzimisces, John I Byzantine emperor; ruled 969–976 CE; consolidated power in the Balkans and Syria.

Vladimir the Great Considered the architect of the Kievan state; ruled 980–1015 CE. His conversion to Christianity solidified an alliance with the Byzantine Empire and brought Orthodox Christianity to Russia.

FOR FURTHER INFORMATION

BOOKS

Kennedy, Hugh. *Mongols, Huns, and Vikings: Nomads at War.* London, England: Cassell, 2002.

Le Tourneau, Roger. *The Almohad Movement in North Africa in the Twelfth and Thirteenth Centuries.* Princeton, NJ: Princeton University Press, 1969.

Martin, Janet. *Medieval Russia: 980–1584.* New York: Cambridge University Press, 2007.

Norwich, John Julius. *A Short History of Byzantium.* New York: Vintage, 1997.

Quigley, Mary. *Ancient West African Kingdoms: Ghana, Mali, and Songhai.* Chicago: Heinemann, 2002.

Tracy, James D., ed. *The Rise of Merchant Empires: Long-Distance Trade in the Early Modern World, 1350–1750.* New York: Cambridge University Press, 1990.

Walker, Paul E. *Exploring an Islamic Empire: Fatimid History and Its Sources.* London, England: I. B. Tauris, 2002.

WEBSITES

Crusades
www.fordham.edu/halsall/sbook1k.html#General

Iconoclasm
www.metmuseum.org/toah/hd/icon/hd_icon.htm

Mongols
afe.easia.columbia.edu/mongols

Ottomans
www.theottomans.org

Vikings
www.bbc.co.uk/history/ancient/vikings

INDEX

Page numbers in **boldface** are illustrations. Entries in **boldface** are glossary terms.

Abbasids, 85, 89, 94
Acre, fall of, 95
Adhemar of Le Puy, 34, 36
Adrian II, 25
Adrianople, Battle of, 6, 103
Aedesius, 129
Aethelred the Unready, 51
Africa, 117–141
  agriculture, 118, 120–121
  early humans in, 117–118
  geography and topography, 119
  languages, 123–125
  social structures, 121–122
  tribes and kingdoms, 127–141
Agaja, 137
Ahmad Baba, 134
Ahmed, 108
Ain Jalut, Battle of, 85, 95–96
Aksum, 127–129

Albigensians, 33, 42, 44–45
Aleppo, Battle of, 85, 96
Alfred the Great, 50–51
Ali, Sunni, 108, 133
Almohads, 93, 97
Almoravids, 93, 130
Alp Arslan, 28, 90–91
alphabet, 25, 67, 125
Althing, 57
Amhara, 128
Anastasius, 8, 10, 14
Anatolia, 8, 11, 20, 26, 28–29, 34–35, 37, 87, 92, 95, 98–99, 101–104, 108–111
Ankara, Battle of, 104
Anna, 55, 67
Antioch, 8, 36–39
Aquileia, Council of, 8
Arabs, 11, 18, 21, 53–54, 91, 93, 96, 101, 106, 110–111, 128–129, 132–133, 137
Arcadius, 5
Ariadne, 8
Arian heresy, 8
Aristotle, 134
Armeniakoi, 18
Ashanti peoples, 127, 136

Askia Muhammad I, 133–134
Askold, 53, 64
Assyrians, 122, 127
Attila the Hun, 7, 7
Augustulus, Romulus, 9
Australopithecus, 117, **118**
Avars, 11, 64
Ayyubid dynasty, 92, 94

Babur, 87, 90
Bachwezi dynasty, 137
Baghdad, 21, 85, 87, 90, 92, 94–95, 97
Bahri dynasty, 94–95
Baldwin of Edessa, 39
Baldwin of Flanders, 46
Bantu, 121, 123–125, 137, 140
Barbarossa, 114
Bardas, 22
Barsymes, Peter, 10
Basil I, 22
Basil II, 26–27, 55, 67
Battle of Adrianople, 6, 103
Battle of Aleppo, 85, 96
Battle of Ain Jalut, 85, 95–96
Battle of Ankara, 104

Battle of Chaldiran,
    108
Battle of Dorylaeum,
    38, 40
Battle of Grunwald,
    73
Battle of Hattin, 41
Battle of Homs, 96
Battle of Kirina, 130
Battle of Kosovo, 104
Battle of Kulikovo, 70
Battle of Lake Peipus,
    72–73
Battle of Lepanto,
    114
Battle of Manzikert,
    17, 27–28, 34, 98
Battle of Mohács,
    111
Battle of Nicopolis,
    104, 109
Battle of Preveza,
    113–114, **114**
Battle of Tannenberg,
    73
Battle of Varna, 105
Battle of Versinicia,
    20
Batu Khan, 68,
    84–85, **84**
Baybars, 95
Baydu, 97
Bayezid I, 104, 109
Bayezid II, 108
Béhanzin, 137
Bela IV, 84
Belisarius, 9–10

Berbers, 93, 125, 130,
    135
Bible, 31, 44–45, 128
Black Sheep
    Turkomans, 99
Bogolyubsky, Andrew,
    65
Bohemond of
    Taranto, 36, 39
*Book of Roads and
    Kingdoms, The*, 131
Boris I, 25
Bornu Empire, 135
Bosporus, 37, 102,
    114
Bronze Age, 122
Bronze Gate, 12
Buddhism, 83–84, 96
Bulala people, 135
Bulgars, 11, 18–21,
    25–26, **25**, 29, 46,
    53, 104, 109
Byzantine Empire,
    5–31
    art and architecture,
        30–31
    later history, 17–31
    Macedonian
        dynasty, 22–26
    rise of the, 5–15

caliphate, 21, 89–90,
    93–94
caliphs, 21, 134
Carolingian Empire,
    52
Cathars, 44–45

Cetshwayo, 141
Chaldiran, Battle of,
    108
Charlemagne,
    19–20, 52
Charles the Fat, 52
Charles the Simple,
    52
Charles V, 114
Christianity, 5–6,
    8–9, 12, 24–25,
    28, 33–47, 49–50,
    52, 55, 57, 66–68,
    81, 92–93, 96–97,
    102–106, 108, 110,
    113, 125, 128–129
Cnut, 51, **51**
Columbus,
    Christopher, 61
Comnenus, Alexius,
    15, 34–35, 37
Comnenus, John, 15
Comnenus, Manuel,
    15
Conrad, 40
**Constantine the
    Great**, **4**, 5–6
Constantine V, 71
Constantine VI,
    18–19
Constantine VII, 20,
    21, 22, 24
Constantine VIII,
    26–27
Constantine IX, 27
Constantine XI, 29,
    105

Constantinople,
5–12, 14–15, 17–21,
24–29, 31, 34–36,
40, 43, 46, 52–53,
55, 64, 68, 72, 102,
104–106, 109
Corvinus, Matthias,
69
Council of Aquileia, 8
Council of Clermont,
33–34, **35**
Council of Nicaea,
8, 18
Council of
Orthodoxy, 20–22
Crimean Tartars, 73
Cyrillic alphabet, 25,
67

Dahomey, 137
Damietta, 46–47
Danelaw, 50–51
Danishmend emirate,
92, 99
de Montfort, Simon,
44, 45
Dingane, 141
Diocletian, 5
Dir, 53, 64
Donskoy, Dmitry, 70
Dorylaeum, Battle of,
38, 40
Dusan, Stefan, 103
Dyophysitism, 8–9

Eastern European
states, 69

Eboracum, 50
Ecloga, 12
Edo peoples, 136
El Bekri, 131
Erik the Red, 58
Eriksson, Leif,
60–61
Ertugrul, 101
Es Saheli, 132
Eugenius III, 40
Ezana, 129

Fanti peoples, 136
Fatimids, 39–40, 92
Ferdinand I, 111
Fifth Crusade, 46
Finehair, Harald, 57
First Crusade, 28,
33–34, 36, 40, 45,
52
Floki, Raven, 57
Forkbeard, Sweyn, 51
Fourth Crusade, 7,
29, 42–43, 68
Frederick I, 42
Frederick II, 42, 46
Frederick III, 69
Frumentius, 129

Gaji, Ali, 135
Galicia, 68
Gaza Empire, 141
Genghis Khan,
68, 70, **74**, 75–81,
84–87, 94, **96**, 97
Germanus I, 14
Gézo, 137

Ghana, 127, 129–131,
136
Ghazan Khan, 85–86,
96, 97
Ghaznavids, 90
Ghurid dynasty, 90
Ghuzz Turks, 90
Godfrey of Bouillon,
36, 39
Golden Horde, 68,
70, 72–73, 84–85,
84, 87, 95–96
Great Wall of China,
78, 81
Great Yasa, 76
Gregory II, 14
Gregory III, 14
Gregory VIII, 42
Gregory IX, 46
Grunwald, Battle of,
73
Guiscard, Robert, 36
Gunnbjörn's Skerries,
58
Guthrum, 50
Guy de Lusignan, 41

Hagia Sophia, **13**, **18**,
30, 31, 106
Halfdan, 50
Hanseatic League, 68
Hattin, Battle of, 41
Hausa peoples, 135
Henry I, 26
Heraclius, 11
Herero people, 124,
140

Herjolfsson, Bjarni, 60
Holy Wars, 33–47
  Albigensian Crusade, 44–45
  Antioch, 37–39
  Constantinople, 43, 46
  Council of Clermont, 33–34
  Egypt, 46
  Jerusalem, 39–41
  Jewish persecution, 35–36
  People's Crusade, 34–35
Homo erectus, 117
Homo habilis, 117
Homo sapiens, 117
Homo sapiens sapiens, 117–118
Homs, Battle of, 96
Honorius, 5
Hulagu Khan, 78, 85, 94–95, 97
Huns, 7–8
Hypatius, 10

Ibn Battuta, 132
iconoclasm, 12, 14, 17–18, 20–22, 30
Idris Alooma, 135
Igor, 54, 64, 66
Il-Khanate, 85–86, 94, 96
Il Milione, 81, **82**, 83
Innocent III, 42–44

Institutiones, 10
Irene, 17–19
Iron Age, 129
Isaurians, 8, 11, 19
Isfahan, 92
Islamic world, 89–99
  Mamluk dynasty, 94–95
  and Mongols, 94–98
  in Northern Africa, 93
  religious tensions, 97
  Seljuk Empire, 90, 92
  spread of Islam, 89–90
  Sufis, 91
Ivan I, 70
Ivan III, 72–73
Ivan IV (the Terrible), 73
Ivar the Boneless, 50

Jagatai Khan, 86
Janissaries, 90, 103, 106, 108, 110, 113
Jerusalem, 33–34, 39–42, 46, 92, 106, 109
Jews, 12, 35–36, 39, 97, 110
Jochi Khan, 84
John of Brienne, 46
John of Cappadocia, 10
John VI, 102

Justinian, 9–10, 12, 106

Kalahari Desert, 118–119, 121
Kanem Empire, 134–135
Karanga people, 137–138
Kayi, 101
Kemalpasazade, 115
Khayr ad-Din, 114
Khazars, 54–55, 64
Khoresm Empire, 79–80, 92, 94
Khumalo, Mzilikazi, 141
Kiev, 53, 55–56, 63–69, 72, 84
Kikuyu people, 124, 140
Kipchak Turks, 95, 110
Kirina, Battle of, 130
Kitboga, 95
Kizilbash people, 108
Knights Hospitallers, 40, 106, 108, 112
Knights Templar, 40
Koran, 91, **96**, 108
Kosovo, Battle of, 104
Krum, Khan,
Kublai Khan, 80–85, **82**, 87
Kulikovo, Battle of, 70

Kurds, 92, 110
Kutuz, 94–95

Lake Peipus, Battle
   of, 72–73
Las Navas de Tolosa,
   93
Lasta, 129
Lecapenus, Romanus,
   22, 24
Leo I, 9
Leo III, 11–12,
   14–15, 17, 19
Leo IV, 17–18, 20
Leo V, 20
Leo VI, 22
Lepanto, Battle of,
   114
Lesbos, 19, 114
Lion of Judah, 129
Louis II, 111
Louis VII, 40
Louis IX, 46–47, 78,
   94
Luba Empire, 138
Lunda Empire, 138
Luo people, 137

Macedonian
   Renaissance, 30–31
Magyars, 25
Mahmud, 90
Mahmud II, 113
Makeda, 128
Mali, 129–130,
   132–134
Malik Shah, 92

Malinke people, 130
Mamluks, 47, 85,
   89–90, 94–96, 98,
   108–111
Mandé people, 130
Mangu, 80, 85, 95
Mansa Maghan, 132
Mansa Musa, 130,
   133
Mansa Süleyman,
   132
Manuel II, 109
Manzikert, Battle of,
   17, 27–28, 34, 98
Marj Dabiq, 111
Masai, 125
Mecca, 130–131, 134
Mehmed I, 104
Mehmed II, 105–
   108, **107**, 112–114
Menelik, 129
Michael I, 20
Michael II, 20–22
Michael III, 25
Michael IV, 26
Michael V, 26
Michael VII, 28
Michael VIII, 29, 46
Mircea the Elder, 109
Mohács, Battle of, 111
Mohammed Shah, 80
Mongols, 65, 68–70,
   72, 75–87, 89–90,
   94–99, 101–102,
   104
   Batu Khan, 68,
      84–85, **84**

Genghis Khan, 68,
   70, **74**, 75–80, 81,
   84–87, 94, **96**, 97
   Kublai Khan,
      80–85, **82**, 87
   in the Middle East,
      85–86
   Tamerlane, 86–87
Monomachus,
   Vladimir, 65, 68
Monophysitism, 9
Moscow, 63, 65, 70,
   72
Moshesh, 140–141,
   140
Mosque of Süleyman,
   115
Mpande, 141
Mstislav, 65
Mughal dynasty, 86,
   90
Murad I, **100**, 102–
   104, 113
Murad II, 104–105
Mwene Mutapa
   Empire, 137–138,
   141

Native Americans, 61
Ndwandwe peoples,
   140
Nestorius I, 9
Nevsky, Alexander,
   68, 70, 72, 72
Nevsky, Daniel, 70
Nicaea, Council of,
   8, 18

Nicephorus, 19, 24
Nicopolis, Battle of,
104, 109
Nika Revolt, 10
Njimi, 135
Nok culture, **116**,
122–123, 129
Normans, 27, 29, **48**,
52
Norsemen, 49–61
Novgorod, 53,
64–65, 67–68, 70,
72
Nubians, 127–128
Nuer, 125
Nur ad-Din, 41

Odoacer, 9
Ogotai, 70, 80, 85
Old Testament,
44–45
Oleg, 53–54, 64, 66
Orhan, 102–103
Orthodoxy, Council
of, 20–22
Osman I, 99, 101–
102
Ostrogoths, 6
Ottoman Empire, 99,
101–115
arts and
administration,
113, 115
dawn of, 101–102
expansion of,
104–105
governance, 110

and Mamluks, 108,
110–111

Pax Nicephori, 20
Pechenegs, 55, 66
People's Crusade,
34–35
Peter the Hermit, **32**,
35–36
Philip I, 36
Philip II, 42
Phocas, Nicephorus,
24
Plato, 134
Polo, Marco, 81–83,
82
Polo, Niccolò, 81
Polovtsi, 68
Prempeh I, 136
Preveza, Battle of,
113–114, **114**

Qarakhanids, 92

Raydaniyya, 111
Raymond of
Toulouse, 36, 39, 45
Red Beard, 114
**Richard I the
Lionheart**, 42
Robert of Flanders,
36
Rollo, 52
Romanus I, 22, 24
Romanus II, 24, 26
Romanus III, 27
Romanus IV, 27–28

Rum, sultanate of, 92
Rurik, 53, 64, **64**, 67
Russia, 7, 24–25,
53, 55, 63–73, 80,
84–85
and Christianity,
66–67
and Golden Horde,
68, 70, 72
rise of Moscow, 70,
72
waning of Kiev, 68
Rustem, 115

Safavid dynasty, 99,
108, 112
Saladin, 41, 92, 94
Samuel, 26
San rock art, 121
Sassanid Empire, 11
Sayfuwa, 135
Second Crusade,
40–41
Sehzade Mosque, 115
Selim I, 108–111
Selim II, 115
Seljuks, 27–29, 34,
37, 39–40, 89–90,
92, 94, 98–99,
101–102
Seventh Crusade, 94
Shabaka, 127
Shaka, 140
Sheba, 128
Shi'ites, 90, 108
Shona people, 124,
140

Sigismund, 109, **111**, 112
Simeon, 25
Sinan, Mimar, 115
Sobhuza, 140
Solomon, 128
Songhai Empire, 133–135
Soshangane, 141
Stauracius, 19–20
Stone Age, 122
Sufis, 89–91
Süleyman I, 110–113, **111**, 115
Sundiata Keita, 130
Svyatoslav, 54–55, 66

Tamerlane (Timur the Lame), 86–87, 96–97, 99, 104–105
Tannenberg, Battle of, 73
Tartars, 73
Temujin, 75–76
Teutonic Knights, 69, 72
Theodora, 21–22, 102
Theodosius I, 5–6
Theodosius II, 7
Theodosius III, 11
Theophano, 24, 26
Things, 57

Third Crusade, 42
Thomas the Slav, 20
Thrace, 11, 26, 102–103
Tonga people, 124, 140
Treaty of Paris, 45
Trebizond, 29
Tuareg people, 93, 125
Tzimisces, John I, 25–26

Ubbi, 50
Ulfsson, Gunnbjörn, 58
Umayyad dynasty, 93
Urban II, 33–34, **35**, 36–37

Varangians, 64
Varna, Battle of, 105
Vasily II, 72
Vasily III, 73
Venetians, 29, 43, 82, 105
Versinicia, Battle of, 20
Vikings, 49–61
  conquest of England, 49–51
  French incursions, 52
  in Greenland, 58

in Iceland, 55, 57
longships, 56, **56**
religion and life, 59
Visigoths, 6
Vladimir the Great, 66–67, **66**
Volhynia, 68

Wadai Empire, 135
White Sheep Turks, 99
Wladyslaw II, 69
Wladyslaw III, 105

Xhosa people, 124–125, 140
Xia, 78, 80

Yaroslav the Wise, 65
Yesukai, 75
Yoruba peoples, 136

Zaghawa, 135
Zangi, Imad ad-Din, 40, 41
Zápolya, John, 111–112
Zeno, 8, 11
Zhu Yuanzhang, 84
Zoe, 22, 27
Zulu people, 124, 127, 140–141